Please, Please
Listen!
This is your body speaking

Please, Please

Listen!

This is your body speaking

Terry Bjelland

To order additional copies of this book, contact:
Xlibris
1-888-795-4274
www.Xlibris.com
Orders@Xlibris.com
772514

I sit here trying to comprehend writing a book. Two years ago, I quit my job and started using some inheritance to spend more time with my business See Your Health. Several happenings in my life the previous five years led me to try a business where I could help as many individuals as possible realize better health. The first was the greatly improved health that I had gained. The second was the loss of my mother and mother-in-law to esophageal cancer. After doing a lot of research, I basically came to the conclusion that they did not have to die as early as they did. In my mom's situation, she had been fighting acid reflux for a number of years. In my research, I found that acid reflux can be reversed with proper care of the digestive system.

I try not to be too negative about the current way the medical field handles our health issues, but my mother did not get the help she should have. My research found that acid reflux can be caused by food not being digested like it should be. My mother was given stronger and stronger antacids to relieve the acid condition. This in no way helped her get rid of the cause of the acid reflux; it only hid the problem. On Dr. Joseph MaCaffrey's website, www.jfmacaffreymd. com, I found the following metaphor that explains how the current medical field operates. My mother was moving along in life and came to this cliff. She was not aware of it and fell over the cliff. There was no medical establishment there to help here. Once she was over the cliff, at the bottom, the medical establishment was there with chemotherapy and radiation. My mother's chance of overcoming esophageal cancer was very low. A medical establishment that would have been there to help my mother would have been at the top of the cliff with help to stop the acid reflux instead of covering the symptoms with antacids.

I am encouraged that some young doctors in the American Medical Students Association are trying to get away from the influence of drug companies on how doctors treat patients. The organization has a branch that has the goal of PharmFree. It is this association that gives me the courage to mention that doctors do not have adequate training to truly help patients with most sicknesses. Doctors have very little training in nutrition. An understanding of nutrition is the best way to help individuals stay healthy and is proving to be the best way to heal most diseases. Hippocrates was the father of natural medicine. His often quoted statement, "Let food be thy medicine and medicine be thy food," is a very profound statement and very true. This is what I feel the doctors should have done to help my mother get over acid reflux.

The first thing would have been to ask my mother about her diet. As I did my research, I came to the realization that almost all diseases are the results of improper nutrition and the damage this does to the digestive system. My mother was also a big coffee drinker and had the coffee pot on all day. This in itself was a big contributor to the acid reflux. My brother and sister said we could have a month to try to reverse this health condition using more natural methods. I remember Mom saying she was having almost no acid reflux at the end of the four weeks. As I look back on this, I am certain she had very little acid reflux because she could not drink the amount of coffee she was used to due to the esophageal cancer. I also believe her diet was better. I share this because this is the reason for this book. A phrase I use often is "If I had known then what I know now, I believe my mother would still be alive". I say this because with the knowledge I have gained from my months of studying and my training to be a microscopist, acid reflux is reversible and does not have to lead to esophageal cancer. The Bible has a verse, Hosea 4:6, that states, "For lack of knowledge, my people parish." My mother was one of those who perished due to lack of knowledge. It is for this reason I dedicated this book to my mother. I want individuals to read this book and gain the knowledge that will help them and motivate them to stay healthy or improve their health. Most cancers and all health conditions can be reversed if the body is given the proper tools to do so. This all has to be done, however, before the body is damaged to the point where it can no longer respond to proper care at the top of the cliff.

On the way to church last Sunday, Gary, a friend of mine, gave me a very good analogy to illustrate the need I have to share the knowledge I have gained so that those who read this book may move to better health. Gary's son had car issues with the battery. Knowing very little about batteries and how to install them, he called his good old dad. Gary did not just give instruction as to how to get the battery into the car but a whole list of things to watch out for to avoid serious problems that may come about if it is not done correctly as well. I am inserting the following quote after I have written most of this book. The quote comes from a true story by Dick Quinn in his book *Left for Dead*. Here is the quote from Mr. Quinn: "When I discovered Cayenne in 1978, I was dying. Cayenne saved my life. It was almost miraculous. With the grace of God and His herbs, I was 56 years old on February 5, 1992. I feel great today, as I have since October 21, 1978. Cayenne has done that for me; maybe it will do it for you. BUT NOT IF YOU DO NOT KNOW ABOUT IT. We are all at risk of a heart attack and we know it. Every day I meet people who have changed their life styles, hoping to live longer. TV ads sell foods with hope. Margarine becomes medicine in the frenzy to lower cholesterol and avoid the heart attack bullet that awaits so many of us. It hit me at 42; it hit my mother at 38. For thirteen years, I have watched the concern about heart attack grow; knowing I have the secret shield everyone is looking for. I am determined to tell you how I beat heart disease, no matter what it costs me. I don't care what you do with the knowledge; I just want you to have it. As a human being, I am obligated to help you if I can. That's why I wrote this. Good luck and good health."

I added this quote because it was just one of many stories about this bit of knowledge that, once found and applied, can save a person's life or ability to enjoy life. Most of the great health books I have studied came about due to the author gaining extra knowledge about health. As a result, their health improved enough to save their lives or improved enough for them to want to continue living. They gained this extra knowledge through self-study, advice from loved ones, or natural health practitioners. This is a good place to list those first books I read that convinced me to change my eating habits and what I ate. I followed some of the changes that were suggested in these books. My health improved and along with it my energy and vitality.

- *The pH Miracle* by Dr. Robert O. Young (I trained under Dr. Robert Young in microscopy.)
- *Natural Cures "They" Don't Want You to Know About* by Kevin Trudeau
- *The Cure: Heal Your Body, Save Your Life* by Dr. Timothy Brantley
- *Cancer Doesn't Scare Me Anymore* by Dr. Lorraine Day (this is a video.)
- *Maker's Diet* by Jordan S. Rubin
- Pushing Yourself to Power: The Ultimate Guide to Total Body Transformation by John E. Peterson

Now that I am motivated to write this book, I will tell you that most of this book will be written from the view of our bodies. I hope that this adds a little more clarity and urgency to the information presented in this book. Now that you have this introduction, let's allow our bodies do some speaking.

Hello there. Let me introduce myself. I am your body. Terry has asked me to help write this book so that you can better understand how I can stay healthy well into old age if I am taken proper care of. I hope that as you read this, you will take this knowledge I will be giving to you and apply it to a better way of taking care of me. I am angry with the way I am being treated by most of my owners. I will try my best not to let this anger affect the knowledge I want you to get from this book. Let's start by giving you some of the reasons why I feel we, the bodies of this day and age, are being mistreated. We are screaming for proper attention. Following are some situations that prove we are being mistreated.

The rise of cancers, heart diseases, and other diseases has been on the rise. We bodies have not changed for hundreds of years, but the way we have been treated has greatly changed for the worst. Unfortunately, a majority of this change is the result of financial gain. Most industries that sell products that have an influence on the body are operating to seek big profits. You, as consumers, have helped. The introduction of fast food and highly processed foods ready for the table has come to harm us. It is true the food you give us today may keep us alive, but it *definitely* does not give us the nutrition to keep us healthy. You as consumers have indicated to these big companies that you are willing support this type of lifestyle. This is a lifestyle where bodies are mistreated for the sake of time and convenience. As a result of this type of lifestyle, we have the SAD diet (Sad American Diet). The United States ranks somewhere around the thirty-fourth in health and healthy lifestyles among industrialized nations, and this figure will vary depending on the sources of information. This one came from the TV documentary *National Health Test*, aired in 2006 in association with USA Weekend. With all the technology of this day and age, we have not added much to life expectancy.

It is true that the infectious diseases have been reduced, but nutritional diseases have now taken over. What are nutritional diseases? Most of the diseases of this current age are the results of what gets into human bodies or the lack of needed nutrients. Terry is writing this book because he has found enough information from his research and has actually talked to individuals that have reversed major health issues, including major diseases like cancer, heart disease, etc., by taking care of me with proper foods and care. We, as human bodies, cannot handle a lot of what is being put through our systems. Equally important is the fact that we are not getting proper nutrition. We would encourage you to go to a website that truly supports the fact that some of us are not getting enough quality nutrition and needed supplements. The website is www.truehope.com. This company was started because a family was able to get a daughter out of a mental health facility by giving her the right combination of vitamins and minerals that reversed her bipolar illness. Terry has found many more examples where proper nutrition and especially high-quality supplements have reversed major health issues without drugs.

We will give you a word of warning when you research natural health information. When a person searches through the web in proximity to a natural product or service, there may be reference to these products as scams. These websites are usually backed by organizations that are against natural health. These organizations are trying desperately to keep natural God-given foods and supplements from getting foothold in the care of us. A good website that will explain why these websites exist is www.quackpotwatch.org.

Another area where we have not received the help we need is from the medical establishments. This may be fighting words for many, but many individuals Terry talked to agree wholeheartedly. Terry feels he has the right to bring out the negative aspects of our current medical practice because so many doctors are doing the same. Nutrition is the key to keeping me healthy, but medical doctors have very little training in nutrition. Terry has found that it may be as little as two weeks or maybe as much as four, but definitely not enough to help them better understand how to make me healthy with God-given healthy foods, nutrients, and supplements.

A young doctor by the name of Jonathan Wright states that he had about one week's study of nutrition. As a young doctor, he tried to use his medical school knowledge to help his patients. After a number of his patients did not respond well to his prescribed medications but did respond to natural vitamins, Dr. Wright began to study vitamins and other natural remedies and saw the body's need for them. The big shock to him was the fact he was not taught this in medical school. He then deliberately looked for a small city far enough from other doctors so that he could use some of these natural remedies along with his conventional treatments. He began to prescribe vitamins and some other natural cures that were not on an approved list of medications. He was even turned in to the American Medical Association by another doctor. This happened to Timothy Brantley when he helped a person get over cancer. Timothy was charged with practicing medicine without a license because he used nutrition to cure a young lady after the doctor had said she would not live. This is in Timothy Brantley's book I listed earlier. Now back to Dr. Wright. As he saw these natural cures truly healing his patients, Dr. Wright began a movement that would help doctors better understand nutrition and its effect on health. For more information, go to a computer and search Dr. Wright. He has a very good newsletter called *Nutrition and Healing* at www.wrightnewsletter.com. As your body, I would urge you to take the advice of well-trained nutritionists along with a medical doctor who is open to the use of natural cures.

Due to the influence of the huge drug companies, the medical field looks to drugs to cure diseases. This movement from natural substances to chemicals for healing started in 1805 when a pharmacist by the name of Friedrich Sertürner discovered morphine. From this discovery began the search for other isolated chemicals that could be used to treat diseases. It is very true that some of these chemicals can work with me, but due to the money that can be made with the right drug, these chemicals are called drugs and are like gold for the companies that can develop them. If you want some very interesting information on the history of the pharmaceutical industry, go to

Wikipedia and search the pharmaceutical history section. Most drugs do not truly cure a disease, only mask the real cause of the disease.

I know that there is a lot of searching for a cure for cancer. Billions of dollars are spent on cancer research. If I were properly taken care of, there is a good chance I would not get cancer in the first place. If I happen to be mistreated and get cancer, I have the capability to get rid of the disease if I am given the proper diet and tools. The biggest tool by far is to give us the proper nutrition we really need. If everyone followed the following principle, I believe I would not have to do much more with this book. The proper nutrition that we need is to eat food as it was originally made by God. In his book, Jordan Rubin talks about the Maker's diet. If you read most of the books I listed earlier, you will find that most of the improvements in health and even the curing of major health issues was the result of eating a lot of foods as close as possible to the way God designed them.

The influence of the drug companies on the medical field has certainly not helped us stay healthy. Thankfully there is a trend by some doctors and hospitals toward treating the health problems of individuals rather that treating the symptoms. An example is a story Terry was told when he went to the bank to get a loan for his business. The loan officer mentioned a friend that was told by a University hospital that he had kidney cancer and had six months to live. This individual went to the best known clinic and hospital in Minnesota for a second opinion. The kidney cancer was confirmed, but the suggested treatment was very different. He was put on a total vegetable diet for two months with no meat and dairy products. We will explain the reason for this later in this book. After the two months were over, his body was in much better shape to handle the traditional cancer treatment. A less harmful type of cancer treatment was used, and this individual was alive many months after the six months passed. He did lose one of his kidneys due to the cancer. I cannot tell you how this individual is doing today, but I believe if he continued with a good diet, he is alive today. I tell this story to suggest doctors and the medical field is changing. My owner has many other stories similar to his.

There are so many things going on in my brain I do not know where to go next. I think I will move to some information that will help you understand some of the so-called foods given to us.

Let's start with pure white sugar. There is so much I would like to tell you about the adverse effects of some of the so-called foods we eat, but that would take away the goal of this book. The goal of this book is to give you enough information so that you will desire to research further the proper way of taking care of me, your body. There is very little nutritional value in sugar. One of the ways sugar does harm us is the way my pancreas and the rest me have to work together. When you consume refined white sugar, it is converted to glucose very rapidly. The blood glucose level rises above what I consider healthy. I then have to have my pancreas produce levels of insulin to help tell the glucose what to do. If I need glucose for energy, I will use it. If the glucose levels are too high, my blood sugar is too high, and I have to balance this out. I regulate the glucose from the blood into a form that will be stored as fat. After years of asking my pancreas to balance blood sugar, my pancreas tends to wear out, and I may become diabetic. The level of juvenile diabetes has become a great concern to all of us. Americans are currently consuming around 180 pounds of sugar a year. No wonder so many of us have not only diabetes but many other health problems. Research is now finding that even levels of cholesterol are also greatly influenced by insulin. Refined sugar has been one of the most harmful substances to have been put through me. Why is highly processed white sugar still on the market? The key is the word market. Certain lobbyists in our government are so strong that politicians do not want to make changes that are so necessary to our health. When there is finally enough negative information about a food substance, the food industry will move to a substitute. Often the substitute is as harmful as the first. With the case of sugar, the substitute is high-fructose corn syrup, which may be more harmful than white sugar. I will suggest often that you look for books that will help you understand some of what I write about in this book. *Sugar Busters* is an example of a book the does a good job of explaining the adverse effects of sugar. It is written by H. Leighton Steward and three medical doctors. I will have a list of other books and websites to go to at the end of this book.

Very similar to refined white sugar is refined white flour. There is very little food value in refined white flour, and I have to deal with it with very little benefit to me. My digestive system has to do a lot of work to get it through the system with no real benefit to me other than helping my owner feel like he has something in his stomach.

A possible tie for a so-called food item that is now being proven to be deadly to us is the use of unhealthy types of fats in our diet. Fats that were a part of God's plan for nutrition are not necessarily unhealthy. The huge problem with fats as they were originally designed get rancid. The food industry, in order to make good profits, had to find ways to stop this. This has led to very unhealthy consequences to us. There are two main issues. The first is the very unbalanced ratio of omega-3 and omega-6 fats. A ratio of four parts omega-6 to one part omega-3 has been proven to cause very little inflammation. When there is unbalance, my blood vessels and heart become highly inflamed. This leads to a lot of health issues, especially heart disease. An open-heart surgeon for twenty-five, Dr. Dwight Lundell has some facts for us. In his book *The Cure for Heart Disease*, inflammation of the heart and the blood circulatory system is the real cause of heart issues. The food industry that provides us with the SAD diet would get rid of the omega-3 due to the fact that this is the fat that gets rancid. As a result, the ratio of omega-6 to omega-3 is around 40:1. The ideal would be around 1:1. This is why we see such a push for quality omega-3 supplements. We will talk about omega-3 supplements later in this book.

The other culprit in dealing with fats is that you are putting hydrogenated fats through my digestive system. These also cause a lot of inflammation of the heart and blood vessels. God's designed fats, such a vegetable oils, butter, and other natural animal fats, get rancid. Take these fats and heat them under pressure to high temperatures, along with the introduction of hydrogen and the use of nickel, copper, or even aluminum-nickel combination, you get hydrogenated fat. This turns out to be a type of cellulose that is very close to being a plastic. Plastic does not get rancid, and therefore hydrogenated fats do not. What a great ingredient to add to our foods. They can stay on shelves for months and allow the food industry to make big profits.

The author of this book is a microscopist; he looks at live blood under a microscope. There are a number of items that can get into the blood that would cause inflammation of the heart and blood vessels. Terry has seen many uric acid crystals and a few triglyceride crystals. Both of these crystals are not nice and smooth. Why do you think gout, which is the result of uric acid crystals, is so painful when they get into joints? They have sharp edges. Even high levels of blood sugar can result in crystals in the blood. These are also sharp. Terry cannot say he has seen plastic in the blood but believes it would be possible to have hydrogenated fat crystals in the blood without being able to see them. At any rate, all these do cause inflammation in the blood vessels and heart. Current research is now indicating that inflammation is the cause of heart disease. Cholesterol gets a bad rap. Recent research seems to show that cholesterol may be in the bloodstream to patch inflamed hearts and arteries. It is possible that cholesterol may be involved in a heart attack, but it is not the reason for the heart attack. The inflammation that cholesterol is trying to patch is the main reason for heart disease. There are several good books that are written to help individuals understand the causes of heart disease and how to prevent and even reverse heart disease. One such book already mentioned is *The Cure for Heart Disease: Truth will Save a Nation* by Dr. Dwight Lundell and Todd R. Nordstrom.

Dr. Al Sears also has a good book, *The Doctor's Heart Cure*. Both books are by doctors who have had a lot of experience with hearts.

It looks like I got a little carried away with this hydrated oil, but it leads to the important issue of heart disease in America. There was so much good information in the two books just listed that I wanted to include in this book. If I begin to include all the information I have on health, Terry would have a book too large to carry. I would suggest you do your own research in natural health for the human body. As I mentioned earlier, Terry will have a list of good sources at the end of this book.

I have just reported on what may be the three most harmful items that are extremely harmful to me. I will now explain a few bits of information that also contribute to my weakening. I suggest that the weakening of human bodies is like the soil erosion of the past. A farming area may have started with twenty inches of good productive soil. Over a number of years, wind and/or water erosion will take the top soil away, and eventually we get down to less desirable soil. This all takes such a slow pace that this erosion is not noticed until it is a big enough problem that agriculture will begin to take steps to slow down erosion with newer tilling and antierosion techniques. This is what has happened to the health of human bodies, especially in the United States.

Going back to the quality of our foods, there are a few things you need to understand about the food you are putting through us. Let's start with something that will surprise and discourage some individuals, especially some of you that have tried to help us by giving us organic food. You have done well to give us food that does not have chemicals sprayed on them or on the soil where plants pick them up. Unfortunately, organic foods may not have all the good nutrition it could have. Let's look at the soil that some organic plants are raised on and maybe most of them. If a plant is raised on soil that has been chemical-free for the required years, it may be free of unwanted chemicals, but it may also be free of all the necessary micronutrients we need and should expect from organic plants. I need in the neighborhood of sixty-two body-usable minerals. The ideal soil would have all these micro- and macrominerals. It is ironic that as my owner was watching an outdoor channel about the top hunting areas for elk, the speaker gave the fact that one of the best elk hunting areas had habitats that had all the necessary nutrients to grow healthy elk. He even mentioned the importance of macro- and micronutrients. How often do we hear about the importance of microminerals in food given to us? Not very often. This leads to some facts we need to know. In 1936, US Senate Document 264 was introduced. This document indicated that our soil was already so depleted of minerals that our bodies should receive mineral supplements. The author of this document had done several scientific experiments that indicated most of the soil of the United States was depleted of many minerals that are needed by the human body. Even organic foods are most likely lacking in adequate minerals and vitamins. When commercial fertilizer is added to the soil, usually only three are mentioned. They are nitrogen, phosphorus, and potassium. What happened to the micronutrients that are needed?

There is a neat little instrument that will help you actually measure the mineral content of fresh plants. It is a brix meter. There are several you can purchase. Let's take a look at ideal soil. Is soil a dead item, or should it be a living source of food for plants? With traditional farming techniques, the soil is dead. When the commercial fertilizers and pesticides are added to the soil, it kills it. It is true this soil may produce higher yields, but at the cost of nutrition. In 1960, US Agriculture began testing the nutrient level of different foods. One example is apples. A person has to eat five apples today to get the same nutrients you would have found in one apple in 1965. This is true for most plants we eat as food. Without getting into too much detail, we can explain what is happening. In an ideal field, soil is continually renewing itself. If you lived on a farm in years past, a lot of you may remember picking rocks out of your fields. The field may have stayed clear of rocks for a few years, and then you were back out in the field picking rocks. In the northern climates, frost action would cause these rocks to come to the surface. If this field is properly taken care of, it will have high levels of microbial and larger living organisms like earthworms that would be able to break down these new rocks into a new supply of health-giving minerals.

There are sixteen different minerals I absolutely need to keep me healthy and sixty-two to have maximum health. Most of these are needed in very small amounts but are very important to me. To have a healthy field, organic refuse from plant and animal sources need to be returned to the field to help the microbial and other living organisms that call dirt home stay healthy. In researching the remineralization of our soils, one suggestion was to find a source of rock dust near your location and spread this on your garden or field. The mechanical crushing of rocks produces this dust. This dust is in small enough size that it is easily broken down into its usable mineral content. These minerals then are used by plants to produce health-giving food, food that I so desperately need to help you stay healthy. This leads me to say that I would suggest that most everyone should be taking very high-quality mineral and vitamin supplements. These quality supplements are not cheap. The minerals in high-quality supplements are plant-sourced minerals. Companies can take a calcium rock, grind it up, put it in a bottle, and call it a calcium supplement. On the other hand, if this same calcium is absorbed by a living organism, such as coral, it becomes something I can use. It is very important a person researches the mineral-vitamin supplements they purchase so that when it is given to me, I can use it to build and maintain health.

The next, and possibly newest, movement to produce high yields and profitable crops is genetically modified foods or crops. Again we are moving away from the way God created food. Like most cases where man-manipulated items are put into or on me, I do not know how to or do not have the necessary chemistry to handle them. My filtering organs like the liver and kidneys are overworked trying to get rid of unknown substances.

Genetically modified foods can be very dangerous. An example was a modified corn plant that could resist an herbicide. This made it possible to use this herbicide without stressing the plant. It soon became evident that this was not health-giving corn due to the fact individuals and animals that ate the corn soon became sick. This corn plant could take up the herbicide into its system and not have a problem with it. The problem for me was that the herbicide was still in the corn. When this corn is put into my system, I do not know what to do with it. As a result, my whole system is weakened and I become sick. There may be some beneficial results to GMO foods, but it is such a new process that little is known about the effects they may have on me. Some countries will not buy rice from United States rice producers due to genetic modification of US rice.

What is the most important organ I have to maintain health and life? There are many parts to the body. We argue often here in the body as to which organ is the most important. One organ that seems to have some good arguments is the blood. The owner of this body is a microscopist trained by Dr. Robert O. Young to understand the importance of blood in the healthy body. Terry will help you understand some of the important functions of the blood that are so necessary to a healthy body.

The first thing to understand is, What does good blood look like? Let's talk first about the red blood cell. A healthy red blood cell is a health-giving cell. Healthy red blood cells are always individual cells. They are nice and plump and perfectly round in shape. They should have a consistent size and color. Below is an example of what my red blood cells should look like. This picture of red blood cells was taken by Terry.

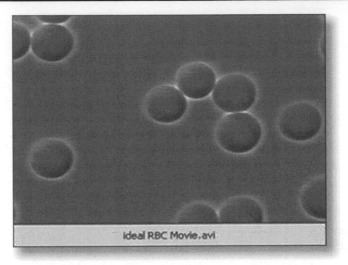

ideal RBC Movie.avi

What do healthy red blood cells do? One of the first things they do is pick up oxygen from my lungs and carry it to my many organs. Oxygen is so extremely important to me. I am about two-thirds oxygen. Oxygen is very important in metabolism. My living cells have a very complicated biochemical process that is called metabolism. The end result of proper metabolism is new tissue being made, energy needed to maintain the body and allow me to move, development of a well-adjusted immune system, and overall good body maintenance. I will make a statement here that is controversial. If I am given the proper nutrition and I get enough oxygen to my body parts, I can stay disease-free. If I do develop a health issue due improper nutrition and poor care of me, I have been created to heal myself if I am provided the proper nutrients and care. The controversial part comes from what I will say now. Cancer and most diseases can be cured if I am given the right combination of proper nutrition and care.

Now back to metabolism. To complete this process, I need a lot of oxygen. Healthy blood will carry up to two hundred cubic centimeters of oxygen. To do this, a red blood cell should look like the one pictured here. I would like to explain how all this works, but I want to keep this book as simple as possible. Terry wanted to know a little more and searched on the computer and found a lot of information.

One site came up as Oxygen and the Human Body. There was a lot of information if you want to go further in your understanding of how oxygen is used by me. Terry has experienced the improvement of my brain function as he improved his diet and began to take quality supplements. He can remember having a problem remembering what tool he was after when he got to the shop where he was working. After His change of lifestyle, as explained earlier, he would be in the exact same situation at the shop but was quick in remembering the tool he was after. His memory had improved enough to recognize the difference. There were many other situations that would confirm better memory. One was the ability to remember numbers when someone would give a phone number. There was not the panic of finding a pen to write down the number. The reason for this improvement in memory was the improved flow of oxygen to my brain. As a microscopist, Terry would check the quality of his blood as he improved his lifestyle and diet. He saw his red blood cells improve. At first, his red blood cells were clumped together.

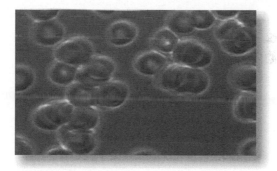

Here you can see red blood cell grouped together. This is not a healthy situation. Red blood cells have to flow through my capillaries one at a time. If red blood cells are clumped, I do not get the maximum flow of oxygen carrying blood to my many parts. The brain is made up of mostly capillaries. With Terry's improved red blood cells, he had better memory.

Very similar to blood carrying oxygen is their ability to supply me with nutrition. Red blood cells must be in good shape in order to carry digested food materials to my parts. Terry will explain a little more about this when he writes about digestion. In the same way, my red blood cells have to be in good shape in order to pick up waste products from my living cells after they do their work. Terry has a strong feeling that a lot of cancer is the result of blood being in such bad condition that it cannot clean up an area of the body that has been damaged by inflammation or toxic situations. In Terry's mother's case, it was the three or four years of acid reflux, a fancy name for sever heartburn that led to the esophageal cancer. If her diet had improved and she could have cut back on the amount of coffee she was drinking, she would have lived a lot longer. For lack of knowledge, we do perish. Please get this into your thinking and consider really looking at how you take care of your body. There is a lot more to the red blood cells and how they function, but in this book, we will try to keep it basic.

Let's move on to another part of the blood. White blood cells are next. They are a very important part of the immune system. White blood cells in the blood flow through the body to clean the blood and watch for unwanted cells. There are five types of white blood cells. Each one has a different job to do. Again, I would explain each white blood cell and their duties but would ask that if you are interested in the white blood cells, search each one on a computer. The five types of white blood cells are neutrophils, basophil, eosinophil, lymphocytes, and monocytes. As with the red blood cells, white blood cells have to be healthy. The most common WBC cleans the blood of unwanted bacteria and waste. It is the neutrophil.

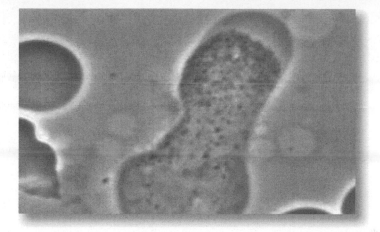

This is a picture of a good, healthy white neutrophil. This cell has its own locomotion and moves throughout the blood plasma to pick up waste. The black dots inside the neutrophil are captured bacteria. The black dot at the lower left of the picture is an uncaptured bacterium. Once the bacteria are captured, the neutrophil will release small amounts of hydrogen peroxide to kill them. When the neutrophil has finished its job, it will break apart and be removed from the blood by the liver. This WBC lives only an hour before this job is completed. The harder the neutrophil has to work, the fewer hours it can work. The liver may get some help from the three other cleansing organs. They are the kidneys, lungs, and skin. An interesting side note is that after a person consumes too much processed sugar, the movement of the neutrophil actually slows down. This means it cannot do as good a job as it could.

The next of the white blood cells is the eosinophil. It is similar to the neutrophil but in much lower numbers. It is not very active unless there is an overabundance of yeast in the blood due to digestive issues and irritation in other of my body parts. Its duty is to pick up larger bacteria and small yeast particles. Less than 4 percent of the white blood cells are eosinophils. The higher levels are found when I have an injury, have had a hard workout, or have had a lot of hard physical work. The eosinophil has a very similar appearance to the neutrophil.

The next white blood cell is the basophil. These are only one-half of a percent of the white blood cell count. They are a smaller size and are found when I am allergic to something. When a microscopist can find a basophil in my blood, it usually indicates there are allergens present and the basophil is active to find these out and destroy the allergen. Basophils are also very important when I have an injury or inflammation. They leave the blood at the site of injury and then release substances that are necessary for healing. This also increases blood flow to the area.

The next white blood cells are the Lymphocytes. There are B lymphocytes and T lymphocytes. The B lymphocytes make antibodies. The T lymphocytes work a little harder. They leave the blood and become T cells when they get to the thymus and mature. They then move to the lymph nodes, spleen, and other tissues where they make antibodies, work with macrophages and neutrophils to fight infection, kill virus-infected and possibly tumor cells. Most of you have heard of the importance of killer T cells. It is very, very important to maintain my immune system so that I can stay healthy. This is done with proper nutrition!

Another part of the blood is the plasma. This is the liquid portion of the blood that allows it to flow though our blood vessels. The plasma should be nice and clean with very little trash. Some of the trash that gets into the blood, usually through damaged villi and poor digestion, are chelated fats, bacteria, yeast, triglyceride crystals, uric acid crystals, lactic acid crystals, and a garbage heap that is a collection of some of the items previously listed. The chelated fat situation is very interesting. As Terry research chelated fat and actually saw chelated fat in some blood samples, he was surprised to find a link between changing the structure of foods to make them better received by the public for more profit and the resulting damage these altered foods can do to our health. When milk became homogenized, it became a product that the public liked better than the milk that had the fat rise to the top. This homogenized process blasts the usually large globules of fat into very small fat particles. When milk fat is left as a fat large particle, it is slowly broken down to be used correctly by me. When this same fat particle is changed to a very small particle by my normal digestive process, it gets to my small intestines and is small enough that it can get through the villi and directly into the blood as chelated fat. This chelated fat actually can cause irritation and damage of the blood vessels and arteries. Then cholesterol has to come along and try to patch these damaged areas. This is a controversial issue since drug companies make such huge profits on cholesterol-lowering drugs. It is Terry's belief and many others that cholesterol is getting a bad rap as a villain. Cholesterol may be the hero, as it tries to patch damaged blood vessels. The crystals mentioned earlier also do a lot of damage to the blood vessels. They have a lot of sharp edges that do the damage.

This is a picture of a garbage heap. It is found in blood plasma that has too much junk in it. This is a collection of bacteria, yeast, and a uric acid crystal riding on top. Following is a picture of living blood with a uric acid crystal.

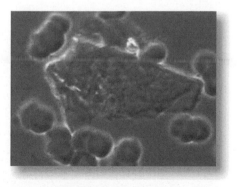

The yellowish white triangle in the picture is a uric acid crystal. It is the result of too much uric acid in the blood. This is often the result of the consumption of too much red meat. Those of you who have had gout know how painful this is. Gout is painful due to uric acid crystals causing irritation, usually in the feet. If you look at this uric acid crystal, you can see that it is not nice and round. It has sharp edges. You can also see why doctors usually recommend individuals with gout to cut back on the consumption of red meat. It is also possible to see that these crystals can cause damage to the blood vessels as mentioned above.

Another area where the overconsumption of red meat and uric acid has a very adverse effect on my heart and vascular system is heart attacks and strokes. With the latest research comes evidence that cholesterol may not be the main cause of plaque buildup in the heart and arteries. Cholesterol may actually be protecting the blood vessels that have been damaged by uric acid crystals and some of the other debris that get into the plasma. This may be triglyceride crystals, which are like broken glass; chelated fats, usually from homogenized milk products; and other junk in the blood plasma. As mentioned before, cholesterol may be patching up damaged blood vessels and, in doing so, do cause blockages in vessels. Instead of taking dangerous cholesterol-lowering drugs, individuals should be changing their diets so that the blood plasma can be clean. With clean blood plasma like that pictured below, blood vessels would stay healthy and would not lead to blockages.

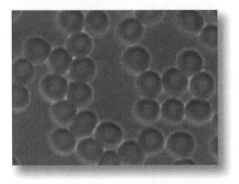

This is a picture of Terry's blood on May 14, 2007. The plasma is clean. That is the area between the red blood cells. In this picture, you can see that Terry's red blood cells are not at optimum health due to the white in the middle. This is yeast as the result of too much sugar and carbohydrates. This was seen very often in the blood demonstrations that were done by Terry.

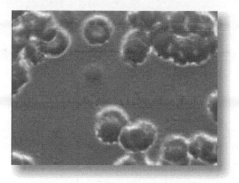

This one last picture has an interesting story. This picture was taken early in Terry's microscopy journey. This picture shows a lot of junk in the plasma and very misshapen red blood cells. The individual to whom this blood belonged to was a very health-conscious person. Terry was trying to figure a way to tell him that his blood was very unhealthy. To Terry's relief, the owner said that he was on a lengthy body cleanse. This explained all the problems there were with his blood. His blood was very dirty because it was taking a lot of toxins out of his body. Some cleanses are designed to do just that. As this individual was sitting there, Terry mentioned that he should be drinking a lot of water. While on a cleanse, individuals should be drinking extra water. The filtering organs often need extra help from the skin to help remove waste. The person that was doing the cleanse mentioned that he was glad Terry had mentioned this since he had not been drinking enough water and had developed some itchy rashes. Rashes are a common symptom that develops during some cleanses if the person does not drink enough water to help move wastes through the liver and kidneys. Some individuals that move to a healthy diet too quickly or start taking a very healthy green whole-food supplement may even move to a cleansing situation and get the idea that they are allergic to the healthy food or supplement. They may even feel that their health has gotten worse. They may even stop their move to better health because they think it is not worth it. This is often the case since I am cleansing and my blood is doing good work. This is called a healing situation or crisis and will usually last about two weeks, in most cases, before I can send to my owner the message that I am doing better. There are many other interesting bits of information that could be added here, but we will move on to another area of health.

With this very short explanation of the blood cells, you can see why it is so important to take care of me so that all these cells can do their part. With the blood, I carry oxygen and nutrients to my other parts, pick up the cell wastes as I keep myself alive, and help me fight off bacteria, viruses, and other items that are not supposed to be in me. If you begin to abuse me with smoking, overuse of alcohol, and most damaging for most individuals, poor diet and lifestyle, I will have a hard time keeping my blood healthy and, therefore, my owner healthy.

So let's move on to the question, How do you keep my blood healthy? My owner would say that the best way to keep me healthy is to eat food the way God created it. That means that we eat food that has not been processed to death. When I say death, I mean just that. When food is changed by processing, it dies. Even the simple process of cooking can kill food. Take a good, healthy, fresh carrot, pea, bean, etc. and overcook it—you basically kill it. This gets us to an area where most people have no clue as to the health benefits of eating as much of their food raw or cooked to low temperatures. If vegetables are cooked so that they do not go over 108 degrees Fahrenheit, they will still have their enzymes active. Enzymes are so important to my health. With enzymes available in the food eaten, my stomach and pancreas do not have to work as hard.

Dr. Robert Marshall, founder of Premier Research Labs and Quantum Nutrition Labs, is a certified internationally trained clinical nutritionist. His web site is www.healthline.cc. He has done a lot of research into digestion. He believes that most individuals have lost the ability to properly digest food due to the inability to produce enough stomach acid and enzymes. Dr. Marshall mentioned a test that can be administered to individuals that actually measure the stomachs pH levels. It is called the Heidelberg test. You can do your own research into this test. There is so much information about hydrochloric acid and the extreme importance of it for good health. A very high number of individuals have low hydrochloric acid levels, and almost all of them do not know it. Most doctors do not have enough knowledge of digestion to recommend good solutions to this problem. When this happens, there is poor digestion. Individuals then have a bloated feeling, belching, flatulence, diarrhea, constipation, and other digestive issues. This then leads to many health issues.

I will again mention the loss of Terry's mother. If her doctors would have understood acid reflux, they should have helped her increase her hydrochloric acid levels instead of lowering them with antacids. Dr. Marshall believes that individuals that have eaten mostly processed foods and especially those that have eaten a lot of fast food will have stomachs and pancreases that have begun to have reduced effectiveness by age forty and even younger. This happens because these types of food do not have the enzymes needed to be digested properly. My stomach lining has to produce high levels of hydrochloric acid, and my pancreas has to manufacture enzymes to try to digest these foods. My stomach and pancreas basically wear out before they should. If you give me foods that still have the enzymes in them, my stomach and pancreas have a much easier time providing the rest of me with high-quality nutrition. My small and large intestines stay healthier if my stomach is able to do its proper job.

Another person that has done extensive research on people groups that have traditionally eaten a large portion of their food raw was Dr. Weston A. Price. Dr. Price was a dentist in the 1930s. He began to see more and more unhealthy individuals with big health issues. He began to ask himself why and became determined to find an answer to this question. The introduction of processed foods had begun, and

Dr. Price felt that this may be the problem. He left his dental practice and began studying people groups that had not moved away from their basic diet of unprocessed and often raw foods. He found that the further away from modern civilization, the healthier the people were. He studied at least ten different primitive civilizations. In a few cases, he could study the primitive people on their usual diet and also some of these people that had become modernized and had begun to eat more modern diets that contained processed foods. In one generation, Dr. Price saw an increase in diseased and unhealthy individuals. He then knew that processed foods were causing the increase in diseased and unhealthy individuals. He had answered his Why question. You can learn more about his work by reading his book *Nutrition and Physical Degeneration*. Another book that may be very helpful would be a book by Robert Bernardini entitled *Everlasting Health*.

My owner has changed his diet, and his health has greatly improved. He has talked a lot about his mother's loss of health but not about his own. Terry was a prime candidate for colon or rectal cancer. Due to his poor digestion, his bowel movements were often very loose and acidic. As a result, there was a lot of bleeding at the anus. Along with this were the very uncomfortable feelings of gas, bloating, and the need to find bathrooms in a short time. This will lead us to something most individuals do not understand or even think too much about. Our bowel movements can tell us a lot about our digestive health. As with our discussion about what good blood should look like, we should know what a good bowel movement should be. A good bowel movement for a healthy adult should be semifirm, close to one and a half inches thick or more, and in a nice long piece. This may all sound too specific, but in Terry's case, it made him see that as his bowel movements improved, so did his digestion and therefore his health. When Terry's diet was poor, there were almost always the very loose bowel movements that were thin ribbons, very acidic, and uncomfortable with burning and itching. How do we get good bowel movements? The answer is to eat a diet that I, your body, can digest food properly. When this happens, I can stay healthy. By far, the biggest thing that a person can do to stay healthy is to eat healthy.

Let us understand why a very healthy diet will do most to help us stay healthy. I think if you really understand how digestion works, you will take better care of me, and I will reward you with the best health you can have. We will start at the beginning. Digestion actually starts even before we get food into the mouth. When my brain realizes I am about to get some food, it gets the digestive process started by telling my saliva glands and stomach to start producing digestive juices. As we take food into the mouth, it needs to be chewed—not just to make the food particles smaller but to start the process of getting the food ready to get into the bloodstream. This is digestion. The food in the mouth is chewed, and saliva is mixed with it. The saliva has digestive enzymes that begin to break down food into usable parts. Terry would like to go into detail about how all this food is broken down to nutrients that the blood can take from the small intestines, but this would go beyond the scope of this book. If a person would like to know some of this information, they can use the computer to research digestion. One site that was of help to Terry was www. phcapsule.com.

Let us continue with the movement of food through my systems. When properly chewed food enters the stomach, hydrochloric acid and other fluids are mixed with the food. When my stomach is healthy, this mixture has just the right acidity and mixture to form a material that is ready to be moved into the small intestines. When this mixture is not right, I begin to have problems or health issues. Acid reflux is just one of the results of an incorrect mixture. A valve at the bottom of my stomach opens when this mixture has the right pH level. If this valve does not open, this mixture stays in the stomach too long and I develop gases and pressure in the stomach that should not be there. It is possible for food to stay in the stomach for up to twenty-four hours. This is much too long. When this happens, this mixture can be forced past the valve at the top of the stomach into the esophagus. You then have heartburn or the new terminology of acid reflux or GERD. Drug companies like these new terminologies because they then are considered diseases. With a condition that is now labeled as a disease, new drugs have to be developed to fight this. This is a very controversial issue. Do doctors have enough training to understand the importance of proper nutrition? As a spokesman for human bodies, I would say absolutely no. Terry's mother was given antacids to reduce the acid in the stomach. This does not help the situation long-term. This may be proper for short-term heartburn.

If you follow the research of nutritionists, we begin to see that instead of antacids, a person with acid reflux should receive something that will help this stomach mixture get to a pH level that will allow this mixture to properly digest and stimulate the valve at the bottom of the stomach to open and let the contents of the stomach move into the small intestines instead of refluxing into the esophagus. One natural remedy often suggested for heartburn was to take a small amount of apple cider vinegar. A professional individual that truly understands digestion will be able to help individuals with many health issues. On the website www.phcapsule.com, the following health issues are most likely caused or aggravated by improper digestion: allergies, skin diseases, osteoporosis, arthritis, diabetes, asthma, anemia gastritis, and even cancer. The website will explain how each of these is possible.

Terry is not a doctor, but as stated earlier, he believes his mother did not get the help she needed to recover from acid reflux. After doing a lot of research, which is possible with the computer, Terry found a lot of information that led him to this conclusion. It is true that there may be some misinformation, but if a person does enough research, they begin to find more and more bits of information that have good sound backing through research. Terry has very little faith in the research results from big drug companies. He will write about this subject later. Following is what I would say is the correct information for individuals with acid reflux. The pH of my stomach should at pH

1 or 2. This acidic condition is created by hydrochloric acid. One important purpose of hydrochloric acid is to kill bad bacteria that get to my stomach through food eaten. This helps us from getting food poisoning. Hydrochloric acid also does some digestive actions. This highly acid stomach mixture works on meats, cheese, fish, and other harder-to-digest foods. It is made up of pepsin, mucin, hydrochloric acid, and a factor that is necessary for the absorption of vitamin B12. Mucin protects the lining of the stomach from the high acidity. Ulcers are the result of low levels of mucin. Pepsin changes proteins to amino acids. As you eat a lot of overly cooked foods and processed foods, my stomach cannot produce proper levels of hydrochloric acid. It eventually gets to a point where there is just not enough to keep my digestive system working properly. Research done with use of the pH capsule has shown that over 30 percent of individuals over age sixty have very low levels hydrochloric acid in the stomach. The solution recommended by nutritionists is to ingest a natural substance that will correct the levels of acid in the stomach. This substance will help my stomach produce the levels of hydrochloric acid that will help me properly digest my food and kill the many bad bacteria that are constantly trying to get into my body. A person should research betaine HCL. This is a highly recommended way to get hydrochloric acid levels to a healthy level so that proper digestion can take place. With proper digestion comes better health!

Once the food mixture in my stomach is just right, the valve at the bottom of my stomach opens and allows the food mixture into my duodenum. The duodenum is the first few inches of the small intestines. Here is where bile from my liver and enzymes from my pancreas should be added to the mixture to raise the pH to a neutral level of pH 7 to pH 9. This neutral pH level is very important for the breakdown of fats into glycerin and fatty acids. Proteins are changed into amino acids. Amino acids are very important to me because they are the building blocks of my body. The small intestines are where I absorb the nutrition that I need to stay healthy. The lining of my small intestines is lined with tiny hairlike fingers, villi, in which blood passes through and picks up amino acids, glycerin, fatty acids, and glucose. These small projections are like the hairs on the roots of plants. They are very delicate and easily damaged. There are several ways they can be damaged. The first may be the result of not chewing food enough. If large particles of food cannot be broken up in the stomach, it is possibly some of these particles can get into the small intestines and damage these villi. This would also happen if the digestive process is not strong enough to get food broken down into proper-sized particles. If the duodenum cannot do its job, the pH of the solution that is passing through my small intestines will be too acidic and damage the villi.

Villi have very few cells between the contents of the small intestines and the blood that is flowing through them. It is here where a lot of unwanted materials can get into the bloodstream. Leaky gut syndrome is one such health issue. Some of the other health issues that happen when my small intestines are not able do what they are supposed to do are poor absorption of life-giving nutrients, acid indigestion, flatulence, and more serious conditions like irritable bowels or leaky gut syndrome. High levels of antibiotics can do a lot of damage to the villi of my small intestines. There are high levels of good bacteria in the small intestines that help maintain the condition of the small intestines. When most of the bacteria are killed by antibiotics, the bacteria called bad bacteria often take over and cause a lot of digestive disorder. A lot of villi are damaged in the process. Yeast called *Candida* get a foothold and cause a lot of health issues. If these conditions are not corrected, Crohn's disease often results. As you can see, it is very important to keep my small intestines very healthy. We will write about what you can do to accomplish this later in this book.

Next in the line of digestion are my large intestines. Once the nutrients I need to stay healthy are absorbed out of the food that is in the small intestines, what is left is passed on to the large intestines. The main job of the large intestines is to absorb water and some minerals out of the remaining food mixture and get it into my system. With proper digestion, my colon will stay nice and clean. With a poor diet and poor digestion, my large intestines become very rough. It will begin to hold poorly digested food, especially fats, and actually begin to stick it to the walls. Poorly digested proteins rot, fats turn rancid, and carbohydrates ferment. This creates an ideal environment for unwanted bad bacteria. Some of these unwanted substances continue to coat the walls of my large intestines until many pounds may be present. Individuals that have done a colon cleanse are surprised at how much of this unwanted waste can be eliminated. These individuals actually weigh less when done with the cleanse. This situation with layers of unwanted waste is very unhealthy. As the large intestines absorb the water through this waste, unwanted bacteria and chemicals are also picked up and enter the bloodstream. This leads to many different health problems. My liver and kidneys are overworked, and the rest of my body has to deal with many unwanted chemicals and substance.

Another problem that may develop in my large intestines or colon would be diverticulitis. This condition was first noticed as populations began to eat more processed foods with low fiber. People groups that have continued to eat more high-fiber raw foods have no problem with this disease. This condition of my colon is the result of high pressure in the colon due to gas buildup and/or constipation. With this high pressure, weak spots in an unhealthy colon will bulge out and cause little pockets to form. My owner can remember a time when he had a portion of his large intestines that had a slow-moving and most likely constipated length of waste. From above, this segment was an area that had a gas buildup. Terry can remember sitting on the toilet for a long time as this gas tried to work past the constipated segment. There was pain involved, and he could feel small amounts of gas getting through so that it could be passed. Any person with an unhealthy colon could have developed diverticulitis or these blown-out pockets.

As long as Terry has mentioned sitting on the toilet, here may be a good time to mention bowel movements. To maintain a healthy digestive system, I need my owner to have at least two bowel movements a day. You may have more or less as days go on, but you should have at least one with two being better. This will keep digested food moving through the whole length of my digestive system at a rate that will allow me to get all the good nutrients out of it and push the unwanted material out of the system before it turns into an unhealthy mass of material. If a person has a healthy colon, the bowel movement should be unforced. I should be able to move the stool out of me without my owner having to pushing very much. The stool should be fairly thick in diameter. This would indicate a healthy colon with nice clean walls.

My owner remembers listening to a CD presented by Dr. Ted Broer. Dr. Broer, before he began to change his diet and health, was amazed at the size of his young child's bowel movement compared to his own. It was a humorous illustration. Dr. Broer's stool was actually smaller than his child's. Dr. Broer's stool was a thinner ribbon due to an unhealthy colon with a lot of unwanted waste. Dr. Ted Broer is another person you may want to look up on the internet for some of his good advice. Another area you may want to search is Dr. Kiromi Shinya and his videos of the interior of the colon. There are videos of healthy colons and videos of colons that are unhealthy mainly due to poor diets. These videos give a person a visual of what happens to one of my body parts when I have to try to deal with unhealthy food items. The unhealthy colons have a lot of fecal material that cannot be moved, very inflamed colon walls, diverticulitis, polyps or small bumps in the colon wall, and other nasty things can be seen. I would like to have pictures of the unhealthy colon in this publication, but it is hard to get permission to print pictures that have copyrights. To actually visualize what unhealthy diets can do to me helped Terry move to a better diet selection.

Terry will interject here that a person can get a lot of information on YouTube. It is on YouTube that you can see Dr. Shinya's videos of the colon. A lot of good information about natural cures for diseases can also be found. You can go to YouTube search engine and type in what you may be looking for. As you look at the material on YouTube, you will have to be selective in the material you want to use. A person can find a lot of websites off YouTube that can present some very helpful information. What Terry has done in his research is to study enough of the different sources of information until there are bits of good information that keep coming up in these different sources that all agree on a bit of information. It was exciting for Terry to find these gems of agreed-upon information. Terry would not have had any idea whatsoever of how he was helping himself move to a very unhealthy old age and an earlier death than necessary if it had not been for one person asking him to go to a mini health seminar put on by a chiropractor. It was the information in this small seminar that started Terry's quest for more knowledge about staying healthy. I am sorry to include a lot of information that comes from the computer since some of you may not use computers. I hope that you will still get good information from this book and some of the books I have listed at the end of this one.

You may now have a better understanding about the extreme importance of proper nutrition and the digestive system. The question now is, How do we do this? The rest of this book will try to help you understand how to have proper nutrition that will maintain a good digestive system. One of the first bits of knowledge a person has to understand is what is good for me. As Terry talks to individuals about what persons should eat to stay healthy, a common statement by these individuals is something like "I could not eat that way" or "How boring it would be to eat that way!" At first, it may seem that way. Dr. Young, the author of *The pH Miracle*, once worked with an actress that had a lot of health issues. Once she became healthy by changing her diet and taking quality supplements, she stated, "Nothing tastes as good as good health feels!" Dr. Young uses this statement often. Why is it so hard for persons to eat what I need to keep me healthy? One of the main reasons is we allow our taste buds to dictate what we want to eat. The best example is the use of sugar or sweeteners. The consumption of sugar has skyrocketed. Soft drink consumption has doubled since 1972. Since 1942, soft drink consumption has increased seven times, and overall consumption of sugar is up three times. The average American eats over 120 pounds of refined sweeteners in one year. Some may say, "How is this possible?" Most of these refined sugars are in manufactured food. Let's look at four examples. In twelve ounces of Pepsi, ten teaspoons; two-ounce candy bar, eleven teaspoons; eight ounces of lemonade, seven teaspoons; and one cup of Kellogg's Frosted Flakes, four teaspoons. It does not take long to get to twenty teaspoons of refined sugar, the average daily consumption in America. The USDA has recommended not more than ten teaspoons per day.

The book *Sugar Buster* mentioned this in the first part of this book, which does a good job of explaining the adverse effects of this high consumption of refined sugars. In very simple terms, my hypothalamus, pancreas, and adrenal glands actually work overtime trying to balance these high levels of glucose that enter my system. It is for this reason we have seen a threefold increase in childhood diabetes in the last thirty years. With the constant battle between the pancreas and adrenal glands, they eventually wear out. Diabetes can be the result. When a person does have diabetes, all refined sugars and even natural sugars have to be controlled. This knowledge you have just received should tell you that it is important to me, your body, to cut out the eating of refined sugars. Even natural sweeteners like honey have to be consumed in low levels.

It is also interesting how the food manufacturers change their labels and ingredients when an ingredient is found to be unhealthy. Before cholesterol was thought to be unhealthy, cholesterol was found on a lot of food labels. Once it was reported that cholesterol may be unhealthy, most processed food labels all of a sudden reported 0 cholesterol. What happened to it? Another thing that food processors will do to appear that they have changed their ingredients so that they appear to be healthier is to eliminate those items that are reported to be unhealthy. Sugar is one such example. What has actually happened is that sugar is commonly replaced by high-fructose corn syrup. High-fructose corn syrup is still a cheap enough ingredient to replace sugar and not affect the price of the food item. The problem is that high-fructose corn syrup may be even more of a problem than sugar. I will try to give you some idea what happens to me when you eat sugar or other unhealthy sweeteners. Most of these sweeteners enter my bloodstream too rapidly. Insulin regulates the level of sugar in the blood. When the blood sugar level rises too high, my pancreas sends out the necessary level of insulin to lower the blood sugar level. The blood sugar level lowers very rapidly due to the form it is in, and I end up with too low a level of blood sugar. My owner then feels very tired and has a lack of energy. To counterbalance this situation, I have my adrenal glands increase the level of adrenaline. This constant battle between my pancreas and adrenal glands wears me out. When the pancreas wears out, you get diabetes.

Another problem I have with too much sugar in the blood is it lowers the amount of vitamin C I can get into my cells. Vitamin C and sugar are very similar in structure, and both try to enter my cells at the same time. When sugar levels are too high, sugar wins out and more sugar gets into my cells to the detriment of my cells and, therefore, my whole system. My immune system is much lower at this time. There are other negative things that happen to me as a result of too much sugar getting into me, but I think you can see why you should eliminate as much sugar and sugar substitutes as you can from your diet.

As long as we have just discussed the adverse effects of sugar on my system, we can take a quick look at processed enriched white flour. To discuss the adverse effect of processed white flour is fairly simple. White flour is starch and will affect me much the same as white sugar. There may be some differences, but basically I will use white flour the same as white sugar. There are some other things with white flour that are not good. When we see enriched white flour, it sounds good. The iron that is used to supposedly enrich flour is a metal and not really in a form that I can use. There are other contaminations that can get into white flour. Terry will not go into these. As a side note, insects that eat white flour will die. You can take a container of white flour and place some crickets or some other insect with a little water so that they do not die from dehydration, and the insects will die. There is nothing in white flour I can use to give me energy or anything of nutrient value. It only makes me work harder to get rid of it without any benefit.

Terry could go on with more, but we think you have received the necessary knowledge to make a move to better health by cutting back on the amount of refined sugar and refined white flour you allow passing those lips of yours. We know without a doubt that you will feel better and improve your health. This is the goal of this book. See why you need to make some changes to your diet or lifestyle, and then do it! How to do it I will talk about later.

Another area that is quite disturbing is the poison that is allowed in foods that can do quite a bit of damage to me. To research some of these poisons that are in your food supply, Terry searched the web by googling in the words *poison in food*. One suggestion came up with hydrogenated oils, poison in food. It was a twenty-eight-page report by the health ranger Mike Adams. Mike is another person who became extremely interested in natural health once he greatly improved his health by going against the traditional recommendations of the current medical advice and moved to natural God-given nutrition and body care. Mike was very unhealthy as a prediabetic and had other health issues. He was under the care of a doctor and was taking medicinal drugs to try to improve his health. He kept getting worse and became very depressed. Someone suggested he should try more natural remedies. Mike began to research some natural remedies and began to apply them to his diet. He began to improve. His doctor was skeptical, so Mike told the doctor that he would continue with this natural health direction and come back after a certain period of time and be one of the healthiest patients this doctor had ever seen. After several months of hard work using natural products and good exercise, Mike went back to this doctor and did as many health evaluation tests they could do and passed test after test on the very high end. He went on to study natural health and natural health supplements and is now one of the best and highly accepted sources of good natural health information. He is known at the Health Ranger and publishes a lot of good information. If you go to truthpublishing. com, you will find good books and reports about health. He also has a good newsletter with a lot of good information, much of it quite disturbing. His newsletter is www.naturalnews.com. Terry includes this information because it supports the statement made earlier that those individuals that greatly improve their health through natural means often become passionate about what has happened to them and they often write books or use some other means to get this information to others.

Now let's get back to hydrogenated oils or fats. These fats are very harmful to me because they alter the structure and flexibility of my cell membranes, which cause a cell-by-cell disintegration of my health. Statistics would indicate that when the food industry started using partially hydrogenated fats in food was when the obesity epidemic began. Any food item that is put into me that I cannot easily recognize gives me a lot of trouble. I do not know how to properly use hydrogenated oils, so they cause me to become unhealthy. The World Health Organization even tried to outlaw this ingredient, but big food company lobbyists managed to keep this from happening. Food lobbyists are also doing this with white processed sugar and high-fructose corn syrup. You can get some very good information in Mike Adams's report on "Poison in the Food" from Truth Publishing on the internet. Also, if you want to stay on top of staying healthy through natural means, and everyone should, go to Mike Adams's website at www.healthranger.com.

Another common additive in a lot of food is MSG or monosodium glutamate. Terry is one person that has a lot of problems with MSG. He used to eat salads at truck stops because he wanted to eat healthy and get back on the road. The problem developed when he was back on the road but had to get back off the road in just a few miles for an emergency trip to a bathroom. To verify his thoughts on salads in restaurants being sprayed with MSG, which his sister-in-law had told him about, Terry went to the website www.msgmyth.com. This discussion board is from ordinary people about their personal problems with MSG. I was surprised at the determination in some individuals to find the additives in the food that they eat. It is very common for restaurants to spray salads with MSG to help keep it fresh looking. Terry also found that sulfites used to be sprayed on salads until several people died after eating these salads. In the 1980s, the FDA banned the use of sulfites on raw foods. A new report states that MSG may be one of the additives in many foods that are slowly poisoning America. Some of the known side effects of this poison are—

Terry had to stop the previous sentence due to the fact that there is a long list of side effects. This list is so long because MSG is known as an excitotoxin. This explains why there are so many different reactions I have to this poison. MSG causes a lot of problems with my nerves and nerve impulses. These result to side effects like diarrhea, flushing in the face, heart palpitations, and many more. Possible long-term damage to me is brain cancer, fibromyalgia, hyperactivity (ADHD), and obesity. It has been recently discovered that the level of your excitement or relaxed state of mind will affect how much an excitotoxin will affect the chemistry of the brain. Aspartame is another example of an excitotoxin and has similar effects on me as the MSG. A book written by Dr. Russell L. Blaylock, *Excitotoxin*, is a good source of information if you want to get more.

As usual, Terry had a hard time getting started writing this morning as he continued his search of poisons or chemicals in our food. There are articles that simply talk about the problems with our food supply to articles that really make a person ask the question, "Why are these poisons and chemicals allowed in our foods by governments?" Terry heard a statement on radio that made him more determined to get this book out to the public. The statement was "What we do not know cannot help us". It could also be stated "What we do not know can harm us". This ties in with Terry's belief in the Bible verse that states, "For lack of knowledge, my people parish." As Terry researched this morning by searching the words *chemicals in our food,* he found even different information than when he searched under *poisons in our food.* This could have been a one- or two-page book. The pages could have been a list of websites to go to that would give knowledge about the problems with our food supply.

Let's get back to the statement that "what we do not know cannot help us". If a person does not know that there are chemicals in our foods that are harmful, then they keep on consuming this food and do great harm to me. A good example is the chemical aspartame and other artificial sweeteners. These chemicals may not be toxic to me, but they still cause me to become fat. This happens because I generally can keep track of the calories I get from natural foods. When I reach a certain level of sweet calories, I signal that we have enough. A person then feels full and will stop eating. With artificial sweeteners, I do not recognize these calories and cannot signal a person I have enough. This person then eats more that he should. This was found with experiments with rats. When rats were fed food with natural sweeteners, they consumed less food than the rats fed artificial sweeteners. The rats who were fed artificial sweeteners gained more weight that those fed natural sweeteners because they ate more. Their bodies did not register that they had eaten enough and overate. This is why most individuals that try to keep their weight down by drinking diet soda or eat food with artificial sweeteners fail. They have a tendency to eat more. This is just one example of knowledge that should help individuals realize that something that sounds good is not always so. Not using as much sugar is good. But because of another problem we have with our food supply, we want taste, so we find something that will still give us a sweet taste. We find an artificial sweetener and feel we are doing something good for health.

This other problem we have with our food supply is the fact that leads back to MSG. As stated earlier, MSG is a flavor enhancer. Many of the chemicals added to our food are designed to make food taste better. Even the many food preservatives are added to make foods have a good taste for a longer period of time. As a result of this, each succeeding generation has to have food that stimulates the taste buds. When young individuals are fed healthier foods, they may not like them because the flavor may be bland or not as exciting. One individual Terry used for a source of information found that his son loved tapioca pudding—the kind bought at a supermarket. This individual saw the ingredients in this pudding. They were not healthy for his son, but they made the pudding taste good. This individual decided to make some good old homemade tapioca pudding with healthy ingredients. His son would not eat it. To him, the homemade pudding was too bland—*not enough taste*. This illustration leads us to what is probably the biggest reason we live in a very unhealthy nation. The food industry is a for-profit industry. That is not the main problem, however. The main problem is that the profit has to be large. Most of the large food companies gamble with our health. Even when companies know that some ingredients are not in the best interest of our health, they use them anyway.

David Burton produced a CD titled *InGREEDients*. In this CD is information on how the food industries have misused partially hydrogenated oils. There is so much more information like this that everyone should look at researching on their own. The computer has allowed us to search almost any topic with much information to be found. If you do not have a computer, the library will have a number of books on food- and health-related topics. Terry searched the computer under the topics like *poison in our foods* and individual items like *partially hydrogenated fats, MSG, aspartame, high-fructose corn syrup, or sugar in our foods*. Terry told you about Dr. Jonathan Wright. When traditional medicine did not seem to be helping some of his patients like he would have liked and found that natural vitamins did, Dr. Wright spent a lot of time in the library researching for more natural cures for some diseases. This illustrates the need for all of us to really research on our own. Dr. Wright now takes a lot of the information that he found and used and is now educating other doctors how to use more natural means to help patients with their health. Please research on your own so that good information is your own and not Terry's or some other person.

So let us move on to some other things you can do to help me stay healthy. Water is an item that we have not covered yet. As we have mentioned often, you need to put things into me that are as near to the way God created them as possible. Water needs to be this way. It would seem that this should be an easy find, but it is not. One would think that if a person lived in a rural area and got their water from a deep well that we would be in good shape. This may be true for most situations, but in these modern days, with the use of synthetic fertilizers and even the use of unhealthy manure, water from wells is not guaranteed to be totally healthy. The most common contamination is nitrite. High nitrite levels in drinking water are most harmful to infants younger than six months. The nitrite turns to nitrate. This nitrate changes normal hemoglobin to another form of hemoglobin that does not carry oxygen. The result is what is called blue baby syndrome. Older infants and adults can change the unwanted type of hemoglobin back to oxygen-carrying hemoglobin, while the infant under six months of age cannot. For this reason, water from wells should definitely be tested for nitrite levels. It is hard to get nitrite out of water. To use water from wells that are not as healthy as they should be, a person needs to filter the water through very high-quality filters, distill the water, or use a reverse osmosis system to purify the water. Even then, there have been some issues with evaporated and reverse osmosis water. These waters may be lacking some essential minerals.

This leads us to the next problem found with drinking water. Most bottled water is not as healthy as we would think it would be. Again the chance to make big profits enters the picture. There are a large number of bottled waters that are no better than regular tap water. The website www.bottledwaterblues.com has a lot of good information. One thing we may not think about is the millions of plastic bottles that have to go to the landfills. Eric Olsen, a Natural Resources Defense Councilor, states that sixty million plastic bottles are manufactured each day and have to be disposed of each day. That is a lot of unnecessary pollution. The best source of household drinking water is water run through high-quality water filters. A person can be assured that the drinking water the family consumes is about as healthy as you can get. You can go to www.watefiltercomparisons. com to find the best filters. If you need to carry water with you, you can refill glass or safe plastic bottles with your own filtered water. This will go a long way in securing your family's health and the planet's health.

Another area you should understand that will help me stay healthy is the area of rest. There is a lot of different information about the amount of sleep I need to stay healthy. Sleep researchers have a name for the situation where individuals basically choose to not get enough sleep. It is called volitional chronic sleep deprivation, and it is a lifestyle disorder. As with a lot of the current research, a lot of good information is being found due to the creation of new technologies. A lot of research on sleep have been stepped up because of one research done by Eve Van Cauter in 1999. Eleven healthy young men were allowed only four hours of sleep for six days. The negative effects on their health were surprising. It was found that these young men were prediabetic and had low levels of the stress hormone cortisol and low levels of the growth hormone. This research was the first scientific evidence that lack of sleep definitely had an adverse effect on me. Most researchers in the area of volitional chronic sleep deprivation say that this lack of sleep is as harmful to me as diet and exercise. It is generally agreed on that I need at least seven hours of sleep to maintain good health. Eight hours is even better.

Terry would like to give you a lot more information on the negative effects of not getting enough sleep, but this book could end up being thousands of pages long if he included all the information he has found on most of the health information he has included in this book. He would encourage all who read this book to research each area on their own. The computer is so valuable to this end. Terry googled in *sleep and health* and got a lot of good information from one website. This site included a lot of other good information about how to take care of me. The site was www.preventdisease.com.

Moving on to another area that most individuals have no idea about its effect on me—the field of electrical influences. It is amazing that there was an awareness of some type of unseen fields that influence the body even hundreds of years ago. The influence of these unseen fields on me is beginning to be discovered. Along with the electrical fields are the magnetic fields. These two fields are very closely tied together. If you think that unseen things do not affect me, you are in for a big surprise. In just the last few years, these unseen fields, or lack of, are causing many health issues. There are a lot of people that know Terry has a passion for helping individuals with their health. He gets phone calls from some of these individuals with information they feel may be of interest to him. One such caller was from a young mother that was very excited about a book she wanted to recommend. The book was by Linton Ober; Stephen T. Sinatra, MD; and Martin Zucker titled *Earthing: The Most Important Health Discovery Ever?* Terry did find some very interesting information. Because of Terry's background in microscopy, he found a section of the book that was using a look at live blood to show that there is a definite possibility that being better grounded to the earth can help one's health. Dr.

Sinatra had three individuals at his house that were interested in this grounding-to-the-earth principle. These three individuals had their live blood looked at before and after being better grounded to the earth using grounding pads for forty minutes. The red blood cells had definitely improved by being much less clumped together. This would definitely improve my health as Terry has explained earlier in this book.

Something else tends to verify that there is an outside electrical influence on our bodies, especially our blood. When Terry has placed a drop of blood on a slide and placed it under the microscope, all the red blood cells are all pulled together in several long ropes, like chains. This is due to static electricity. Once the static electricity dissipates, the red blood cells begin to separate and Terry can proceed with the evaluation. This would lead us to believe that the unseen presence of unseen electrical fields have an influence on our bodies. One illustration that may help us understand the importance of grounding is the need for lightning rods on buildings, especially the old type of wooden buildings. If lightning were to strike a building that is not properly grounded, it can actually explode and/or catch fire. There is so much force in the lightning strike. If this same building has a lightning rod that is properly grounded, the force of the lightning follows the lightning rod and the grounding wires into the ground and the building is protected. Trees have no lightning rods, so when they get hit by lightning, they usually explode in some form and are scorched by the heat. All this is mentioned here to say that this idea of grounding ourselves as completely as we can whenever possible can improve our health. The book mentioned above has some very interesting information. They suggest a person, whenever possible, go barefoot when walking to truly be grounded to the earth. Another suggestion is to purchase grounding pads to be used when sitting. By placing your bare feet on these pads, you are better grounded and some health benefits result.

Another unseen field of influence on our bodies is the magnetic field. The magnetic field and electrical field are very closely tied together. One very good website to do your own research is www.drpawluk. com. As Terry continued to write, he has realized if he included all the interesting information he has accumulated, this book would lose its purpose. This book is to provide enough information to get individuals to realize the importance of understanding the extreme importance of how the body works and how this modern world and its influences have been an enemy of the body. As stated earlier, most of the authors of books that are about helping people understand how to improve health as it should be improved—*naturally*—have greatly improved their own health by such means. Speaking from Terry's body's point of view, I am so happy he got interested in understanding how I work and did everything he could do to help me be healthier. He still has some things he has to work on, but I am doing so much better. I have more energy, my brain is better able to store and recall information, my digestive system is working much better, and much more. My badly broken ankle twenty-some years back has become less painful instead of more painful as I get older. This sounds like the conclusion of this book, but it is not. It is just a reminder to myself why I have been encouraging Terry to write this book. So many people could move to better health if they could just get enough information to spark an interest in taking care of their own bodies.

As Terry speaks to as many people as he can, there are an increasing number of people who are aware that the current medical system is not working, our government is not truly working to protect us, and we need to get back to nature and understand how the body works and take care of it gently and naturally. Terry has mentioned that the body has many assets to properly digest food. There are lactases, protease, maltase, amylase, lipase, and others. There is no such thing as chemicalase. When we put chemicals into us, we have a hard time knowing what to do with them. This includes prescribed drugs. We manage to direct these chemicals to different organs to process them, but we usually get harmed by doing so. The liver is one organ that really gets overworked. If you listen to some of the drug commercials and the side effects of these drugs, one or two statements stand out very often—"Liver damage may be a possibility" or "Have your liver tested before you take such a drug". The purpose of the liver is to cleanse the blood. If I get too much unnatural solutions into my system, my liver has to work overtime. When these unnatural chemicals go through my digestive system, they disrupt my healthy way of breaking down food. Often poorly digested food gets into my blood, and the liver again has to work overtime to clean the blood. You will again hear a very common statement with the side effects of different drugs—you may get diarrhea or have an upset stomach. Again, all this is being mentioned to encourage individuals to really question the use of drugs and chemicals I do not know what to do with.

It is here where I can mention a neat organization that is encouraging doctors to distance themselves from the drug companies and their influence on how doctors treat patients. This organization is the American Medical Student Association. A website that is a part of the AMSA organization is www.pharmfree.org. Here you will see that there are a large number of medical students that realize that the drug companies have too big of an influence on medical care. There is a large amount of information on this website that will help individuals realize that they should maybe question their doctors on the use of drugs. Here is where I can again ask individuals to google for information on natural ways to correct a medical situation. Terry has a T-shirt from the AMSA that has the word *PharmFree* on the front. He shows this to audiences when he has done health seminars. He then asks these individuals where he got the shirt. To answer the question, Terry turns to the back of the shirt. On the back is the American Medical Student Association. This surprises a lot of these individuals. It has given Terry courage to help individuals question some of the suggestions doctors may make with health care. Please go to the PharmFree website to get some very interesting information.

As Terry began to write this morning, he realized if he kept on writing about all the very interesting knowledge he has learned over the last six years, the book could end up with thousands of pages. He has many books, computer-printed pages from hundreds of websites he has researched, and probably best of all is the information from individuals he has talked to. These individuals have encouraged Terry. He knows he is on the right track. To move toward the completion of the book, Terry will try to review how the body should work and then how to help it work properly.

As soon as we are conceived, I have to take in nutrients. In the womb, I get my nutrients from my mother. Please excuse me here because I am already getting off track. Proper nutrition for pregnancy not only keeps the mother healthy but also gives the growing infant the best possible chance to enter this world at as close to 100 percent as possible. I guess this would be another book. To stay healthy, you have to *absolutely* put nutritious and healthy food into me. When that happens, I stay very happy. We will start at my mouth. When I get the message that I am about to receive food, I begin producing saliva to mix with this food that is about to enter my mouth. This is most likely where the phrase *mouthwatering* comes from. This food then has to be chewed well so that there are no large chunks of food that will enter the rest of the digestive system. These larger chunks of food can cause problems. First, the stomach does not have enough churning action to break these down. Second, these large chunks of food are too large to allow the digestive enzymes to properly break them down. The TV program *MythBusters* wanted to see if Coke would dissolve a steak. The Coke did not totally dissolve the steak but made it very soft and almost digested. The steak was a whole T-bone—not a very realistic test. If they had ground up the steak and then added the can of Coke, it would have been a different outcome. I believe the steak would have been liquid. The same principle happens in the stomach with large chunks of food. This is even true with chunks of raw vegetables like carrots. *Chew food very well!* Next, improperly digested food chunks can move into the small intestines and damage the very delicate villi that line the walls of the intestines. This causes my liver to have to work hard to cleanse the blood of improperly digested food. As these larger chunks move farther down the digestive track, they may even begin to rot and cause digestive upset and gas and slow down the digestive process. Whenever this happens, the large intestines begins to allow unwanted bacteria and yeast into the blood system as it absorbs water from the material that is within.

Now back to properly chewed food. Food that is properly chewed has started the digestive process by predigesting some of the nutrients in the food. You then swallow the food, and it enters my stomach. The stomach then churns the food and mixes in the hydrochloric acid it has produced. This strong hydrochloric acid not only digests food but also kills unwanted pathogens that could cause food poisoning. Also added are some digestive enzymes that begin to break down food into small particles that can enter the bloodstream through the villi in the small intestines. The lining of the stomach has mucosa cells that produce mucus that protects it from the strong acids. When the contents of the stomach have the correct acidity and the digested food is properly mixed, the valve at the bottom of stomach opens and allows the contents to move into the first part of the small intestines. If the contents of the stomach do not reach this ideal condition, the valve may delay opening. This causes a number of health issues. The main one is the one that led to Terry's mother's esophageal cancer— acid reflux or heartburn. The food stays in the stomach too long and may begin to ferment. This fermentation results in gases and other types of acid that create an acid reflux condition. Surprisingly, not enough hydrochloric acid is a big reason for the delayed opening of the lower valve of the stomach. Terry has already covered some of this earlier in the book.

Once the stomach has released its contents into the first section of the small intestines, the digesting food's acid level is greatly reduced to a neutral level. If it were to stay highly acidic, it would do a lot of damage to the very delicate villi of the rest of the small intestines. Again, you can see that improper care of the digestive system could make it possible for this to happen. With this digesting food properly mixed and moved into the rest of the small intestines, pancreatic enzymes and bile are added to the mixture. The pancreas and liver are important at this point. They are the producers of the pancreatic enzymes and bile. Bile's main purpose is to digest fats. Pancreatic enzymes break down the carbohydrates and proteins. Once this happens, the digesting food has been broken down into micronutrients that can pass through the walls of the villi into the blood that is flowing through them. The villi are like the root hairs on plants. They are only one cell in thickness. You can see why it is so easy to injure these villi. A website that does a great job of explaining the villi and what health issues develop from injured villi is www.becomehealthynow.com. Go to small intestines under the body heading. There you can see how damaged villi can lead to a number of diseases. The autoimmune line of diseases may very well be the results of damaged villi and/or the small intestines. This is possible because some of the intestinal content that would not normally get through the intestinal lining does and gets into my bloodstream and lymph system. I do not recognize these particles and treat them as foreign matter. My immune system kicks in and battles them as enemies. When this continues for a long enough period of time, my immune system gets worn out, and we have the autoimmune type of diseases begin to take over. The abovementioned website does a good job of explaining this. Another site is www.everydayhealth. com. Read the article "What Is Leaky Gut Syndrome". Now back to a healthy discussion. When my small intestines are healthy, the food eaten has now been broken down into the micronutrients that will be used by the rest of my systems and organs. The rest of the material moves on to my large intestines.

The main purpose of my large intestines is to absorb the water out of the digested material that has reached here. This digested material is also mixed with more friendly bacteria and mucus so that it is reduced to feces, which is then ready to be expelled. It usually takes about thirty-six hours for this all to happen. This is a good time to explain what a good bowel movement should be like. This is all very important because a person can tell a lot about the health of their digestive system by their bowel movements. First, a bowel movement should be semifirm and all together in one main piece. With this good bowel movement, a person should have to use very little toilet paper. The bowel movement should also be self-moving. That is, it should be automatic with very little or no pushing. It should also be fairly wide. This means that in most adults, it should be about one and a half inches or more. The reason this is important is that this is about the size of a healthy large intestine and rectum. My colon should also be nice and flexible. Terry remembers Dr. Brower's funny story about his surprise at the size of his young daughter's bowel movement. It was bigger than his usually was. This leads to an important health issue that develops if you do not maintain a healthy diet and digestive system. When Dr. Brower did a number of colon cleanses, he found that his bowel movements did increase in size. The reason for this is that the large intestines had gotten rid of a large amount of terrible waste that had coated his large intestines and had become more flexible. A man that did one of VE Iron's seven-day cleanses weighed some of the toxic waste that came out of him, and it weighed fourteen pounds. A very good website with information about colon cleanses is www.detoxifynow.com.

In 1956, Mr. Irons spent six months in jail and paid a $6,000 dollar fine for refusing to follow the FDA's order to stop making his health statements about the colon cleanse. After his release from prison, Mr. Irons helped start the National Health Federation. Terry realizes that there is so much information about different natural health products that it is hard to decide what to use. He would suggest that you keep on looking until you find a website like the one mentioned here. Mr. Irons was truly a person who had the health of individuals as a lifelong goal. He was ninety-eight when he died, not from disease but in a car accident. We had better get back to the importance of a healthy colon. When I have a lot of toxic waste that lines my large intestines, I have a hard time maintaining healthy blood and health in general. As the water is absorbed through the large intestinal wall that is coated with this toxic waste, it also will pick up the toxicity of the rotted food, unfriendly bacteria, and other chemicals that are staying in the colon too long. As with the small intestines allowing unwanted materials into my blood, the large intestines have done the same. Now my blood cannot do the best that it can do, and my liver, kidneys, lungs, and even my skin have to work overtime to try to cleanse my system. These are my purifying systems.

Here is a good time to mention such things as bad breath, very smelly flatulence, and body odor. All these troublesome body issues are most often the result of poor digestion. Even body odor is the result of the body getting rid of toxins that should not even be there. My skin is often called the third kidney. A person that follows a healthy diet and lifestyle will generally have very little body odor. When you do a strenuous exercise or work up a sweat, the fat that is near my blood vessels will begin to release some of the many toxic chemicals it has stored to keep them away from my other body parts. These chemicals are then released to my lymph system and carried to my sweat glands. If there is an overabundance of these chemicals, I will begin to have unhealthy skin issues. If a person can sweat often enough to keep these toxic chemicals diluted as they leave as sweat, skin issues will be less. One way to sweat on a regular basis is the use of saunas. Of course, the best prevention is to eat healthy so that I do not have to store the toxic chemicals in the first place. A lot of bad breath is the result of poor digestion and not just poor toothbrushing. This bad breath can come from the stomach and the lungs. The lungs can help me get rid of some toxins. Whenever a person starts on a healthier diet or begins to take good, natural health-giving supplements, this person may get very frustrated if they do not know about what is called a healing crisis. If I have had to store toxic wastes in my fatty tissues and my owner begins to eat very healthy foods or takes these natural health supplements, I will begin to get rid of these toxins. This person does not know that they have actually started a cleanse. This leads to what is called a healing crisis. I recognize that my blood and lymph system are clean enough to start getting rid of some toxins, so I release them. When this happens, I need to have my owner drink a lot of water to help move these toxins out of me. As these toxins move throughout the rest of my systems, my owner may feel less healthy. Many individuals that do not know this give up on eating healthy or taking some very good supplements. This healing crisis will usually last about two weeks but varies to the type of cleanse that is taking place.

Terry again found some very good information by doing a search under the healing crisis. The site he found the most helpful was www.the-natural-path.com. This healing crisis is one area that has caused a lot of misunderstandings when a person, without proper knowledge, tries to help me be healthier and gets into this healing crisis. There are many individuals that will spread wrong impressions about trying to be healthy when they try something and it does not work. Terry knows of several cases where a person was encouraged to try a good supplement and gave up after a short time because they said they felt worse. Once they received the correct information and continued on with the healing crisis, these individuals began to see the very positive results they were told they would receive. These people then became believers in healing me with quality food items and supplements that I can understand and use. Leonardo Da Vinci made the following statement: "Vitality and beauty are gifts of nature for those who live according to its rules." Another phrase that was used in a commercial for margarine was "It's not nice to fool Mother Nature". Terry wanted to know the exact statement, so he googled in "It's not good to fool Mother Nature". All Terry wanted was the correct statement, but he got more. He found one lead that was as follows: it's not nice to fool Mother Nature!—age of autism. This ended up being a very good article about autism and how vaccines are a very possible contributing factor that leads to autism. It was a very good article on this modern controversy. We will not go into this area of controversy.

Another area similar to the vaccine controversy is the mercury issue with amalgams in dental work. I should have encouraged Terry to include this information in this book, but that would be in another book. It was just interesting how Terry found some very interesting views on how trying to fool Mother Nature has created a large number of problems. This information was found on www.ageofautism.com. The article was "It Is Not Nice to Fool Mother Nature". Mr. Da Vinci's statement about nature and following its rules to get to vitality and beauty are very true. Terry got a little sidetracked here, but he has found so much new information as he uses the computer to search for more knowledge.

Terry has already mentioned the issue with misinformation that the medical establishment seems to give out. Terry was having a friendly discussion about health issues with a small group of men at a coffee shop. As mentioned earlier, Terry talks to as many people he can about basic health. The topic turned to diverticulitis. Terry stated that this condition is most often the result of diet. One of the men said that he had asked his doctor if what he ate was a contributing factor to his diverticulitis. This doctor gave this individual some very bad advice and said that diet had very little to do with diverticulitis. Diet has everything to do with this condition. Again, we emphasize the fact that doctors get very little training in nutrition. Terry has been surprised at the number of individuals that want to deny that what they eat is important. This individual may have misunderstood the information given to him by the doctor. Diverticulitis happens when a person is constipated due to poor diet. With poor diet, the walls of my large intestines become weak in some areas. When my large intestines are blocked by a harder-than-usual bowel content and has to be forced forward, the area above the blockage will build up unhealthy pressure. There is usually pain and bloated feelings. If the unhealthy large intestines have weak spots, this pressure will cause the wall to bulge out. This is diverticulitis. This will especially happen if a person eats something that produces a lot of gas and this gas cannot get past the blocked area of the large intestines.

If this doctor told this individual that diet has nothing to do with diverticulitis, he was wrong and possibly caused this individual a lot of unnecessary pain and medical costs. A person has to eat properly to maintain my healthy large intestines and healthy bowel movements. We need to eat foods with a lot of fiber to do this. Here is where eating good-quality raw vegetables can do wonders.

Terry has spent a lot of time and words to try to help you understand the importance of keeping my intestinal system healthy. With a healthy digestive system in place, the most important organ, the blood, can do its work. When the blood can do its work, the rest of me can maintain proper health. As a microscopist, Terry understands the extreme importance of healthy blood. After doing hundreds of demonstrations, it was clear that those individuals that maintain a healthy diet have healthier blood. These individuals had very few, if any, illnesses. If a person maintains a healthy diet and keeps my blood healthy, it is actually hard to get sick. Most of the major diseases currently causing so much trouble have come about near the start of the 1900s. This is when we began to process and overprocess food. Preservatives and other chemicals began to be added to foods. A little later, fast foods became popular. The latest and newest attack on food is the genetically modified foods. Food has almost become nonfood. In 400 BC, Hippocrates made the following statement, "Let food be your medicine and medicine be your food." Thomas Edison made this statement: "The doctor of the future will give no medicine, but will interest his patients in the care of the human frame, in diet and the cause and prevention of disease." If the abovementioned statements are true and a lot of our food has become nonfood, we are in big trouble. Persons who would be following the advice of the statement above have had to change the way they talk about food. These persons have to add a word before food. This word is *functional*. We then have functional food. Functional foods are the foods that these two men were talking about. The good old-fashioned foods, now called functional foods, that were nutritious are no longer easily available.

With the disappearance of easily available quality food enters the need for another way to get the necessary nutrients into my system. Just to illustrate this need, I need at least sixty-two minerals to stay at peak health. There are sixteen minerals that are an absolute necessity. As stated earlier in this book, it was mentioned that our soils have been depleted of most minerals. Terry was very curious about what was in the US Senate Document 264 and found it on the web. He was surprised at what he found. This document was the result of Congressional study on US farming practices. Most of the information given was put together by Dr. Charles Northen. He specialized in digestive disorders and nutrition. As he studied, he realized there was very little good information on how quality nutrition could be used in the medical field to cure or help individuals stay healthy. He and a French scientist began to study minerals and their importance to healthy plants and, as a result, healthy animals. This included humans. Dr. Northen began making statements about the need to take additional mineral supplements to stay at optimal health. He was severely criticized about these statements because it was a common belief that we would almost always be able to get enough minerals from our foods. Some of Dr. Northen's research can be found in this document.

In a ten-year study with rats, it was found that if a family of rats did not receive enough calcium, they would become irritable and would not get along with one another. When they were then given enough good-quality calcium, they became less irritable and would actually go back to sleeping together in a nice pile. There is a lot more good information in this document. Look up US Senate Document 264 and read it yourself. What is ironic is that the Congress realized the cost of getting our US soil into better shape would be high. All the information was swept under a rug and never acted on. This document was dated June 1936.

Let's move into the modern world. With the introduction of the new technology called biofuels, a lot of crop residue like corn stalks and straws will be made into fuel. This means that we are withdrawing minerals from the soil and not putting any minerals back into the soil. Nitrogen, phosphorus, and potassium are the only minerals that are actually being added back to the soils at high levels. No wonder our soils are depleted. Even our organic crops may be very deficient in minerals. Many organic farms can become qualified to be organic after only a few years of rest without the use of chemicals. This is not enough time to build soil with a good mineral base. Good-quality research has found that if I do not get enough quality minerals, I will have a hard time fighting off diseases and other health problems. As Terry has done his research, he has found that most of the leading natural health supplements come from areas of the globe that have not had large commercial agriculture. The rain forests have always been the leading source of natural healing supplements and foods. One of the best-known ancient remedies where a food item became medicine was the use of oranges and lemons onboard oceangoing ships. A Scotsman by the name of James Lind worked his way up in the medical ranks to become one of the top medical persons in the navy. He had been researching scurvy and found that those sailors that had consumed lime or orange juice did not get sick. He published his findings, but very few took his information seriously until Captain James Cook took Dr. Lind's findings and implemented them. Captain Cook did not lose a single man to scurvy during his circumnavigation of the globe from 1768 to 1771. Dr. Lind died before his recommendations were fully implemented in 1794, forty years after he had originally made them. Again, this is an example of an early use of food as medicine. What follows is a modern interest in food as medicine.

Terry will now surprise everyone with what he is about to introduce to you now. He is very excited about what he has just found this morning. In his research for modern information on food as medicine, Terry found a website that made me jump for joy. The search lead that came up on Google was "Food as Medicine: Powerful New Drug Could Be at the End of Your Fork". The website was www. ultrawellness.com. The title of the blog was *Food as Medicine*. There is a video by Dr. Mark Hyman that is about the most exciting bit of information Terry has found. It definitely gives a person hope that we are moving in the right direction. It is about an exciting shift in the medical field, especially some doctors, toward recognizing nutrition as an extremely important necessity in the prevention and cure for disease, even the major ones. Let's hope that these new ideas about food as medicine moves forward faster than Dr. Lind's ideas did.

Following are some of the stories Terry has heard as he talked to individuals about health.

One of the first was a friend of the family that had a small cancerous lump on her breast. After doing some research, she began using natural foods to fight off this cancer. In her case, she read a Baptist pastor's account of becoming cancer-free by using natural foods. This pastor was George Malkmus and is now doing health seminars all over the United States.

While working on his job, Terry talked to a turkey producer that told him about a neighbor that had cancer and juiced a lot of carrots and was able to fight off the cancer. He drank enough carrot juice that his skin turned a slight orange, but he was alive.

While taking his aunt to the airport, they got to talking about health and healing diseases with food. She told Terry about her grandfather's fight against a major disease. It was most likely cancer. He was able to stay alive by just eating grapes. He did this for a few years before he gave up and began eating other foods. He died a few years later. If he would have had some additional information, which is the purpose of this book, he may have been able to vary his diet and still fight off the disease he had. The natural product in the grapes' seeds was most likely resveratrol. Resveratrol has been found to be a very good natural product that has a very positive affect on health.

An even more exciting story was presented to Terry at a coffee shop where he has his once-a-week treats. The owner of the shop gave him a small book written by a local mother that had been given acne medication while she was pregnant. This led to some very serious health problems for her eighteen-month-old son. This young lad developed stomach cancer. He was given chemotherapy, but doctors told the family that the cancer was too aggressive and the child had a few months to live. The family knew of a chiropractor that believed strongly in natural medicine. He and the family were able to talk to one of the child's doctors to put a tube into the child's stomach so that they could administer high quantities of fresh carrot juice and some high-quality vitamins. To make the story short, this young lad became cancer-free. At age seventeen or around this age, the owner of the shop's daughter was still in contact with the teenager. The title of the book is *Your Child Doesn't Have To Die!* by Leanne Sorteberg. Terry just checked with Amazon.com to find the correct spelling. There are books that can be purchased.

While going to a large church in the Twin Cities, Terry helped start a health resource group. One of the other individuals that helped start the group was diagnosed with a small cancerous lump in her breast. She began seeking natural means to cure her. She ended up in Eau Claire, Wisconsin, with a naturopathic individual that did provide a way to fight this cancer. The cancer was cured. This individual was a very active member of the health resources group. We had one meeting in which three other individuals had beat cancer with all natural means. One of Terry's goals is to work with churches to help members become knowledgeable in the better care of their bodies. I get very excited about this. Most individuals are just not aware of the fact that they are not taking care of us.

While in a café, Terry was talking to the waitress about being healthy. She was already eating a lot of vegetables because a coworker had been diagnosed with prostate cancer. He was determined to avoid surgery. He did not want a cancerous tissue to be cut into, which he thought could help the cancer spread. He did some research and began a very healthy diet with a lot of vegetables. He was able to beat the cancer!

While doing some short live blood demonstrations at a chiropractor's office, one gentleman had come in that had been on six or seven drugs for his heart. He had found another chiropractor that had helped him with nutrition and other excellent supplements. He was able to get off five of the drugs with his doctor's approval.

While giving a presentation for a company that produces quality supplements and cleaning supplies, Terry listened to the story of a young lady that had been in a mental hospital in Canada with bipolar disorder. Her father was at church helping with a project when he talked to a fellow worker about his daughter. This fellow happened to be a feed formulator for an animal feed supplement company. He knew of a condition in swine that was similar to bipolar disorder. This condition was easily corrected with the right minerals. They decided to put together a similar package of human-grade minerals to see if it could help his daughter. They tried this mineral supplement on this father's son. The son had begun to show signs of bipolar disorder. The son responded very well to this treatment, so these minerals were introduced to the daughter in the mental hospital. What is ironic is that this mineral supplement had to be given to her secretly because this was not an approved medication and would not be administered by the hospital. She made a very dramatic improvement and was soon released from the hospital. You can read about the story in her book *A Promise of Hope*. This young lady's name is Autumn Stringam. You can also google in Autumn Stringam and hear more of her story.

There are other stories Terry has heard but thinks these are enough to help readers realize that there is a lot that can be done to improve one's health or, better yet, maintain good health. If you multiply the number of stories Terry has heard in his little world by thousands, we begin to see that there is the beginning of awareness that we bodies can be taken better care of if our owners only had good knowledge on how to do it. Again, the purpose of this book is not necessarily to give you this knowledge but to push readers to the point that they can grab a hold of the concept that we can be healthier and stay healthy if we research how. Terry never would have believed the amount of material that is available to individuals to help them be knowledgeable about taking care of their bodies.

At this point, Terry realized he has not filled you in on his own improved health. As Terry began to realize there was more that he could do to be healthier, he began to take better care of me. His path to better health started when his mother-in-law was diagnosed with esophageal cancer. And yes, Terry's mother, Irene, was diagnosed with the same cancer within months after Lillian's. Both were lost within one year. Terry's wife, Pat, went to a small health seminar put on by Lonnie Holmquist, a local chiropractor. Part of the seminar was presented by a company that was started by Dr. Robert O. Young, the author of *The pH Miracle* and the individual that trained Terry in microscopy. Pat purchased a super greens product that Dr. Young had developed. Lillian was supposed to drink at least three quarts of this green drink but could not because of the cancer. Irene had the same situation and could not drink enough of the drink to help. Terry began to drink close to three quarts of this green drink each day. He was determined to give it a fair try. Prior to this, he had a serious digestive situation. He had figured, like a lot of individuals, that it was due to his age of fifty-seven. After taking the green drink for about one month, his digestion began to improve. Terry continued to go to the mini seminars and began to get some very eye-opening information on healthy living. This is when he began to study how to properly take care of me. I responded by digesting his food properly, and Terry started to have healthy bowel movements without the diarrhea and bleeding. I was at a high risk of developing colon or rectal cancer. Terry was a truck driver and had a miserable time in the truck as his digestive problems raised their ugly heads. As his digestive issues disappeared, he began to enjoy not only his job but also life in general.

At one of the meetings at Holmquist Chiropractic, it was mentioned that Dr. Young was asking for individuals in Minnesota to come to California and study to be a microscopist. Terry and Pat had been to two microscopists and were totally fascinated with the ability to look at their own live blood on a computer screen. He was able to see the improvement in his live blood as he had improved his diet between the two microscopy sessions. It looked like it was too financially out of reach, but Pat and Terry prayed for God's will and help. Prayers were answered in a strange way as Terry rolled a pickup on icy roads in January of 2005 that produced a totaled-out pickup that provided enough cash for an opportunity to go to California. Terry attended the microscopy training in February of 2005 and began doing some microscopy sessions. The unbelievable knowledge and understanding he gained made him determined to help as many individuals as he could understand the importance of nutrition in maintaining a healthy *me*! In 2007, Terry opened his business as See Your Health. He was determined to teach others some of the important basics of keeping their bodies healthy or getting them healthy if there were health issues. Partly due to lack of business skills and training, Terry's two attempts at local health seminars failed. Probably one of the biggest mistakes was the idea that there were a lot of people who would be interested in improving their health. Those few that did attend were very supportive of the idea. They would have liked to see more. Some said that they would try their hardest to get friends and relatives to attend the next seminar, but due to finances, no more seminars were scheduled. Another area of great frustration for Terry was the fact that he could not open an office and do his microscopy demonstrations. Because a drop of blood is taken, this could be considered a medical test and a person could be accused of practicing medicine without a license. Individuals that had been doing microscopy in other states have had their computers, cameras, other equipment, and all records confiscated by federal authorities. Terry went back to work with his brother to build up the finances and regroup. After continuing his conversations about natural health with as many individuals as he could who would listen, and there were many, the idea about this book developed after two individuals suggested he should write a book. After a number of conversations with a young medical student, Terry mentioned that he was writing a book. When Terry had a conversation with this same student the following week, he was encouraged because this student was wondering when the book would be finished. He said he would have to be patient and give Terry a chance to finish it.

Now that you have a little history, back to writing more on helping the body stay or get healthier. Another area of physical health that greatly affects me is the way my mind is trained. I admit that the mind is a complicated part of me. Terry has no training when it comes to the mind but has some information that may be helpful. The Bible continually speaks about the body, mind, and spirit as one. Proverbs is a book of the Bible that is about wisdom and knowledge. "A joyful heart is good medicine, but a crushed spirit dries up the bones" (Proverbs 17:22). In this verse, we have an idea that a person that will make every effort to keep a joyful attitude will be healthier. A joyful heart is good medicine. The way my mind works has a lot to do with how joyful my heart will be. The good medicine would be endorphins. Endorphins are released in my brain into my bloodstream to be carried to all parts of me. These endorphins help all parts of me to be more relaxed. Endorphins will also reduce pain. When you exercise me, I release endorphins into my system. Exercise is very important in keeping me healthy. It is the endorphins that are released during exercise that helps me be more relaxed and often gives my owner a feeling of well-being after exercise. Of course, exercise is also very important to me because it helps use up excess calories and keeps my various parts in good shape. A website that has a lot of very good information is www.helpguide.org. Just go to the healthy living section to get a lot of material. One of the choices is Body, Mind, and Spirit. Please go to this website because Terry would be writing a lot more pages he does not have to if you use some of the web information found on this site. The following information about the above website is written as Terry neared the end of writing this book. He had gone back to the site to find some more information about stress when he found information on why this website was started.

The creators of this site created the help guide after the loss of their daughter to suicide. Like so many of the very good sources of excellent health information, those who write books or start websites do so to get the much-needed knowledge about true health to as many individuals as they can. Following is a statement from their website. There is a lot of good information on this site:

> Helpguide was launched in 1999, following the suicide of Robert and Jeanne Segal's daughter, Morgan. We believe that Morgan's tragedy could have been avoided if she had access to well-written professional information that gave her a sense of hope and direction. Helpguide is focused on providing free online resources that are motivating, balanced, and ad-free—easy to look at, easy to understand, and focused on information you can use to help yourself.

An area that greatly affects a person's health is how a person handles stress. This is another area that is very complicated, but with good knowledge, there comes a correct handling of stress. For Terry, this is something he thought he could not write too much about but realized he has had sixty-three years in which to experience plenty of stressful situations. Part of the reason Terry thought he could not write much about stress was that he has been able to handle the stressful situations well and they do not haunt him after the stress has been handled.

The reason it is hard to write about stress is that a lot of the effects of stress on me, the human body, are complicated by a number of factors. In Terry's case, he was raised in a very loving family. Every person will have a different story, and everybody has a different way of handling stress. This is where Terry can give his suggestions on how he handles stress and some very good sources to go to get good information. There are differences in everybody that are inherited. Some individuals will be able to handle stress very well, and others will not. Terry has been one of the luckier ones since he is a very calm individual that handles stress well. He believes this is due to the way he was raised, his inherited nature, and his relationship to God. Some individuals may not agree with the following suggestions, but these have been used successfully by many individuals. Terry will fill you in on how this works. Terry became a born-again Christian when he was a freshman in college. The very helpful concept that comes from the Bible is that God really cares for us and wants to take care of us. The verse 1 Peter 5:7 states that we should "cast all of our cares upon him because he cares for us". Terry also believes that God is perfect and does not make mistakes.

In 1986, Terry slid off the roof of his house and broke both ankles. While lying in the hospital waiting for his surgery, he was very stressed because for the next four months, he would not be able to work. He had a very small disability policy with large bills and an insurance office to pay for. As he tried to work his way through the stress, he remembered 1 Peter 5:7, so he cast his cares on his best friend. Terry also new that God was perfect and that God does not make mistakes. Many of you would say that that was a mistake—who would benefit from broken ankles, especially when one was in very bad shape and would cause pain for years to come? Terry would say that it was not a mistake due to two main results of the injury. As a result of this injury, Terry has been super careful in most of the physical work he has to do. He has to do a fair amount of climbing ladders at work. He always uses the three-point principle that involves the use of three stable points. This means you use two hands and at least one foot or a combination of three limbs while a person is climbing or in unstable situations. This has kept Terry out of a lot of trouble. The second positive result of the accident was that Terry had to be home for his preteen son and daughter. Selling insurance at the time kept Terry away from home many evenings. Terry's being disabled for four months kept him home and him needing a lot of help. His son and daughter were very willing helpers, and the family benefited from two broken ankles. A third benefit of this accident was seeing that natural remedies can help. While watching TV in the late 1990s, a glucosamine product began to be advertised as a product that could help repair joints and relieve pain. Terry began using this product, and it did greatly improve the comfort in his ankle. It took several months before the improved comfort was felt, but there was a definite improvement. Proof was found when glucosamine was not taken for a few weeks and the pain began to come back. This is all being presented to you to possibly help you see that God is perfect, and it may be hard to see how this is possible in most troubles we may go through. Terry's family has had other situations that were hard to figure out, but after looking back, they saw that many of the hardships usually led to positive outcomes. This way of handling stress may seem like a cop-out. When stress hits a person, just hand it off to God. To do this, however, a person has to have a loving relationship with his Heavenly Father. Our Heavenly Father does want us to cast our cares on Him. He is big enough to handle our situations and there for reduce our stress. This is one of the best natural means of handling stress. There are *no* drugs that can do this. Please give your Heavenly Father a chance to help you with your stress. Not only is this a temporary solution, but it can be a permanent solution if you accept Him as a personal friend and He will carry you to a permanent residence in heaven. This section of this book is somewhat out of context, but it is included because it is a large part of Terry's well-being. If this can help just one person to healing, it is worth the space in this book.

Now we can get back to the effects of stress on me, the body. As mentioned earlier in this book, the body has a lot of balancing to do. As Terry has continued to do his research, he has been amazed at how many situations in the body have to be balanced. To give you a little review, following are some of the balancing acts that I have to accomplish to stay healthy:

- pH balances (The blood especially has to be balanced to stay at a pH of 7.3.)
- Omega-3 and omega-6
- Calcium and magnesium
- Zinc and copper
- Body temperature
- Hormones
- Good and bad bacteria (This is correct. We need some bad bacteria.)

When we begin to understand how stress affects me, a person will begin to realize how important it is to try to control stress. When the person who owns me allows stress to continue for an extended period of time, my health is negatively affected. When I say a person allows stress, that is what I mean. Due to lack of knowledge, most individuals do not try to control stress. They may believe they are just normal and stress is a normal part of life. Stress is a good thing in some cases. Examples would be if you are in a dangerous situation, stress will help you get out of this situation. Stress can help a person get a project finished if there is a time schedule. The right amount of stress in an athletic event may help performance. The same is true in performing arts. When stress begins to affect health is when it is not allowed to be a part of a person's daily routine. When stress is a continuous part of life, health will be negatively affected. Stress is a flight-or-fight mechanism. I respond to flight or fight by releasing these hormones. The correct balance of stress hormones is no longer in balance. These hormones get my heart beating faster, and we get higher blood pressure. My muscles tense, and my mind goes into high gear to respond to this stressful situation. This is the result of the hormones that I release into my system to get out of trouble. This is all okay if it is for a short period of time. When stress is allowed to continue for extended periods of time, the listed results of the flight-or-fight mechanism drain me. This is called chronic stress. My brain, nervous system, and other organs are damaged. This damage is at the cellular level. Glutathione is my naturally produced antioxidant. Antioxidants are very important in battling the breakdown of my cells due to oxidation. With long-term stress, my glutathione level gets very low, and my immune system is greatly weakened. I end up with different situations in my systems called disease or sickness. The antioxidant is one very popular supplement you are encouraged to take by individuals that understand how I work. These can be taken in a supplement form or by eating the right kind of foods that have high antioxidant levels.

As Terry continues to write, he continues to do research. There is so much information that individuals who read this book may want that cannot be put into one book. The computer has allowed Terry to find very good sources of information. For this section of the book, two websites were found that had possibly some of the best information about stress and the immune system. The first is www.stress-affects-health.com. Linked from this site was the restore-the-immune-system website www.digestaqure.com. These sites had a large amount of great information about stress and other information on how to keep me healthy. This is again the main reason for this book — *to give you the necessary information so that you have the knowledge to take better care of me, your body.* Please take the time to study some of these websites. Again, Terry apologizes if you cannot use a computer. If at all possible, find someone who will help you get this information from a computer, and you two individuals may gain the knowledge necessary to improve health. A book Terry just found that is extremely well-done and is totally dedicated to antioxidants was written by Carlson Wade. It is *Eat Away Illness: How to Age-Proof Your Body with Antioxidant Foods.* In this book are very specific supplements and foods high in antioxidants. Terry was not going to include specific information on the many needs that I have, but I encouraged him to do so in this case. He googled for foods high in antioxidants and went to the website www.suite101.com and found the following top foods in order: small red beans, wild blueberries, red kidney beans, pinto beans, cultivated blueberries, cranberries, artichokes, blackberries, prunes, raspberries, strawberries, delicious red apples, Granny Smith apples, pecans, sweet cherries, and plums. The top supplements are vitamin C and selenium in high enough levels that will help me.

A question many individuals have is, What is the correct amount of vitamins and minerals to take? Another website that was helpful is. www.wdxcyber.com/ngen21.htm. The RDA or recommended daily allowance for vitamins and minerals is a very low level. These levels were set just to prevent deficiencies. In most cases, much higher levels have been found to greatly help improve my health. One example is vitamin C. The RDA for vitamin C is 60 milligrams. There is some very good research that points to levels at around 1,500 to 3,000 milligrams as a level that will actually help me maintain health.

This now leads Terry to wonder about the recommended levels of medications that are given. Depending on the health of my digestive system and overall health, I have quite a range of abilities in taking nutrients into my system and also the speed at which nutrients are taken into my systems. Terry recognized this difference after leaving the dentist's office. After Terry was given a medication to numb his mouth, it would take about forty-five minutes for the numbness to work its way out of his mouth. This was before he changed his diet and began to take high-quality supplements to improve his health. About a year after he began this program to better health, he was back to the same dentist. He was again given a numbing medication. This time the numbness was gone in about twenty minutes. Some would say that it was the amount of medication given or the type of medication given that it disappeared from his system faster. I would say that this could be the reason, but I believe it was due to the better condition of Terry's red blood cells. They were able to carry the medication to the filtering organs to get them out of the blood and out of the body very efficiently.

Another similar illustration was from a person that was giving a presentation to an audience about being healthier due to a supplement she was taking. She was a wine drinker. After several months on this nutritional supplement, she noticed that the effects of the alcohol in the wine was hitting her sooner than it used to. Why was this? I believe, again, that it was due to the improved circulatory system. Her blood was carrying the alcohol through her system faster, and as a result, she noticed it sooner. This leads Terry to ask some important questions about the different responses different individuals may have to medications and even good supplements. The two extremes would be a person whose digestive system is so damaged that it cannot take up the medications or supplements to a digestive system that is very healthy and can easily take up the medications or supplements. In the first situation, a doctor prescribes a medication with the assumption that it will be taken up by me and used. This person would not get the results intended. The same is true for good-quality supplements. Terry has been told by persons that have tried a good-quality supplement that they did not see any or very little improvement in their health. The possible reason, either temporary or ongoing, may be the condition of the digestive system. A person with a poor digestive system would have to stay on a health-improving supplement for a much longer period of time to give his digestive system time to improve to a point where the supplement could do its job. If a person takes a good-quality supplement with a very good digestive system, he or she may experience a healing crisis as explained earlier in this book. A person should always give a supplement at least two weeks before deciding if it works or not. Terry is very convinced that *the digestive system is the key to great health*. This was seen as true as Terry improved his diet and then saw improvement in his digestive health that led to some other health improvements.

After reading this book to this point, a person should now be convinced that there is a lot that can be done to help reverse a health issue or to prevent health issues and stay healthy. At this point, I will try to give you some specific information to do just this. This will be done by following a food item through my digestive system. This food will be as close to the way God created it. We can take a salad with spinach, cut-up raw vegetables, and a seasoned olive oil dressing. We will follow this food throughout the digestive process. Let's get it started.

You are hungry, so the digestive process has already started with saliva being produced. Already, you may have some problems if you do not have enough saliva or the saliva does not contain some of the enzymes necessary to start breaking down the food. Following are some situations that would cause poor saliva production: drinking or eating food that has too high a temperature and food items (I would question if some items are actually food) that have chemicals that I do not know how to handle or may damage my saliva-producing glands. When you have the food in your mouth, it is very, very important that the food is chewed enough so that there are no large chunks of food. One suggestion to help a person spend more time chewing food would be to put down the fork or spoon after each bite. Chewing food well is a habit that is very important to develop. It is a habit that everyone should work on. Chewing food adequately is the key to having the food in small enough pieces so that you do not damage the lining of my stomach and especially the villi in the small intestines. The pieces of food also need to be small enough so that they can be broken down into small enough particles so that the digestive juices in the stomach and small intestines can prepare the nutrients in the food to be absorbed into the bloodstream.

The partially digested food is now moved from my mouth to the stomach by the esophagus. Once in the stomach, the food is mixed with hydrochloric acid and the enzyme that breaks down protein. Also produced is a substance that protects the lining of the stomach from the acidic condition. The lining of the stomach produce these. If my stomach is not taken care with good-quality food and a person controlling as much stress as possible, the following problems occur. Ulcers can develop due to the lack of protection for the lining of the stomach. Heartburn or acid reflux disease, as the drug companies like to call it, is a common problem. This problem of my stomach needs to be corrected and not covered up with antacids. An occasional antacid may not be a problem, but continued use is. As stated earlier in this book, there has to be enough hydrochloric acid in the stomach to properly break down the food. Correct levels of hydrochloric acid also protect you from foodborne bacteria that can cause food poisoning. The enzymes also have to be available. With the consumption of highly processed foods and fast foods, my stomach very often becomes overworked, and it cannot produce the needed levels of these digestive juices. As a result, I have trouble moving the partially digested food out of the stomach and into the small intestines. The contents of my stomach have to be in the right condition before the valve between the stomach and small intestines will open. When the contents of my stomach are not released in a timely manner, they become overly sour and more damaging as acid reflux when it does escape back up into the esophagus.

With proper diet and lifestyle, food empties my stomach in a timely manner, and it is in the best shape to be handled by my small intestines. The bad bacteria are killed, there are no large food particles that have not been broken down, and there is a correct acid-and-enzyme content that will help my small intestines do its major job. The major job is to break down the food particles into nutrients my bloodstream can pick up and move to the liver. We will get to the liver after the small intestines. The small intestines need help and get it from the pancreas, liver, and gallbladder. My pancreas produces the enzymes that break down fats and proteins and get them into my small intestines where they can go to work. The liver sends out bile so that the digested fats can be moved into my bloodstream through the one-cell lining of my small intestines. My gallbladder stores the bile until it is needed. When all these elements go as planned, I get all the nutrients I need to stay healthy. It is so extremely important to me that everyone understand this. If a person really understands how my digestive system really works, they will do their hardest to eat properly and maintain a relaxed lifestyle. When a person does not have the knowledge stated above, they have no clue that they are causing themselves a lot of pain and suffering. This pain and suffering come in the form of disease. I will try to cover some of these.

Acid reflux and stomach ulcers are found when my stomach is mistreated. When my small intestines are mistreated, there are even more problems. The lining of my small intestines is lined with tiny hairlike fingers that allow the digested food to pass around them. Because of these villi and microvillus, the surface area of my small intestine lining is greatly increased. These villi are very delicate since they are one cell thick. They are similar to the root hairs of plants. Once these villi are damaged, a lot of health issues develop. One would have a very fitting title. The issue would be leaking gut syndrome. The research into leaky gut syndrome is becoming very important. Once thought to be important to only individuals interested in alternative medicine, the field of traditional medicine is beginning to take interest into the possibility that a leaky gut is possible and this will lead to health issues. A lot of the new autoimmune diseases are now looked on as a possible result of leaky gut due to damaged small intestines and their villi. These villi are very easily damaged in different ways. The first would be when you do not chew your food enough. When large pieces of undigested food get to the small intestines, they can scrape along the walls of my small intestines and damage these villi. Toxins and many food additives are chemicals that I do not recognize, and they will be passed along these villi and damage them. One class of very damaging chemicals is the antibiotics. With high use of antibiotics comes damage to the villi and the loss of good bacteria that are so valuable to the health of the intestinal tract. Good bacteria are very necessary to keep the bad bacteria at low levels and also to aid in the breakdown of food. It is highly recommended to take high-quality probiotics if it is absolutely necessary to use an antibiotic. It is very important to have a correct balance of good and bad bacteria. Eating foods with a lot of preservatives will also throw off this balance. The preservatives are put into the foods to kill bacteria. Just because these chemicals are swallowed does not mean that they will not kill bacteria. They can kill good bacteria in the digestive system.

VITALITY AND BEAUTY ARE GIFTS FROM NATURE FOR THOSE WHO LIVE ACCORDING TO ITS LAWS. (LEONARDO DA VINCI)

Another situation that will cause a lot of issues with my small intestines would be the extra time that material would have to stay there. If my owner does not have at least one or, better yet, two bowel movements a day, the material that is in the small intestines can start to decay and produce more and more damaging bacteria. Yeast and fungus begin to develop. Some of the major digestive disorders are then able to get a foothold. Crohn's is one of these conditions. Celiac disease is another situation that can develop. This is a condition where a protein in wheat, barley, and rye triggers the immune system to attack the villi of the small intestines. In these cases, a person has to avoid these grains in their diet. As Terry mentioned before, a proper balance of acidity and alkalinity are very important. If the digestive fluids that enter the small intestines are too acidic, the villi can be damaged. If the fluids are too alkaline, there is less damage to the small intestines, but food will not be properly absorbed. One last situation that develops in my small intestines over a long period of time when an unhealthy diet and lifestyle are followed would be the filling in of the spaces between the villi. This allows a place for bad bacteria to work. It also reduces the surface area of the small intestines where food can be absorbed. A person will tend to overeat because they can feel hungry. This is true with some of the other issues that cause the absorption of food to be decreased. To review, a nice clean small intestine will allow the correct mixture of food and digestive aids to move past the healthy villi. The correctly digested food groups are then correctly broken down into components that the body can use to stay healthy. These components then pass through the villi and into the bloodstream, where they move to the liver. Here the liver prepares these components for distribution to the rest of me. I am then very happy. If I receive a proper diet and care through a good lifestyle, I can give my owner years of good health well into the golden years of one's life.

Once this mixture of food and digestive aids has reached the end of the small intestines, most of the nutrients have been extracted from the mixture and it moves into the large intestines. The large intestines are not quite as complex. My large intestines' main purpose is to absorb water from the mixture that just came out of the small intestines. As it does this, it will also take with it some of the nutrients that are still available. Good bacteria are again a major contributor to the proper function of the large intestines. These good bacteria properly break down the rest of the nutrients that have gotten past the small intestines and start preparing this mixture for elimination. They also help keep the unwanted bacteria at bay. This is extremely important in the large intestines due to the length of time this mixture has now been in the digestive system. The condition in this nice, warm, and moist environment is ideal for bacteria to grow. When unwanted bacteria overcome the good bacteria and take over, many health issues develop. Many of the autoimmune diseases are a result of this takeover. Too many unrecognized items get into the blood system and body tissues. These unrecognized items confuse my immune systems, and my protective system of guard cells that make up my immune system will attack parts of me that they should not. We get the word *autoimmune*.

Again, Terry spent a large portion of his morning writing session doing more research. He is totally amazed at the amount of information he finds on the internet. He is also very encouraged with this morning's information because it was from two women that had an autoimmune disease and basically did what Terry is trying to do with this book—get individuals to realize that a lack of knowledge on their part may be keeping them from the best health they could have and the possibility to live a healthy life right up to the moment of death. The two sites that Terry found were put together by two women that basically got over their autoimmune disease by researching the causes of the disease themselves and following the suggestions and knowledge of proper diet and lifestyle. Again these two women found that the traditional medical system does not address the cause of autoimmune diseases and therefore could not help them. When they got the knowledge concerning some of the base causes of their disease, healing began. Hope for these two began to grow, and they now pass on this knowledge to others. The two websites are www. evenbetterhealth.com and www.autoimmunity-bible.com.

Now back to my large intestines. When the following conditions develop in my large intestines, health issues do arise. Already mentioned is the overgrowth of unwanted bacteria. As these unwanted bacteria grow, they produce unwanted chemicals and other substances I do not want. Over a period of time, usually years, a large amount of this sludge will attach to the walls of my large intestines. This unwanted material causes my large intestines to be very inefficient. It cannot do the job that it is supposed to. It is at this point some individuals would recognize the thought of getting rid of this buildup. This is where there would be a discussion of doing colon cleanses. A colon cleanse is where an individual will use natural herbs and supplements to help loosen this buildup. We will not take a lot of time here to discuss colon cleansing, but there is a lot of information on colon cleansing. At least you have the knowledge that keeping the colon clean will greatly improve your chances for the best health.

The other issue with a lot of rotten sludge in my large intestines is the fact that this sludge will contain a lot of toxic chemicals from the foods eaten. These chemicals will come from food, medications, and the toxins from dead bacteria and fungus that will be in this sludge. What makes this such a problem for me is that the water that is being drained out of the newly digested food passing through my large intestines has to pass through this sludge to get to the lining of intestines. A lot of really bad stuff goes with the water into the blood system. My filtering organs have to work overtime to try to get rid of these toxic wastes. Some of these wastes are not recognized by the filtering organs and get moved to the other parts of me. It is fortunate for me in this situation that some of these wastes can be pushed into my fat cells where they will not do as much damage. As I become more and more toxic, I often use fat to protect myself of these toxins, and my owner gains weight.

Some individuals that become aware of the natural care of me, their body, become aware of ways to cleanse me of these unwanted wastes. One such person that decided to do a cleanse was mentioned earlier in the book. It is the last picture of what can be found in live blood. It is the picture of very poor live blood with a lot of misshapen red blood cells and the plasma is carrying a lot of filth. As Terry was doing this blood demonstration, he was not sure how he was going to tell this person, who was actually following a healthy lifestyle and diet, that his blood was very dirty. When this person mentioned that he was doing a cleanse, Terry was thankful to find this out. He was able to tell this person that the cleanse was working. When a person does a cleanse, the blood becomes super clean and can then begin to take in some of these toxins that have been stored in the fats. During a cleanse, a person can feel slightly sick. My blood becomes toxic for a short time and is not as efficient as it should be. Once over a cleanse, I am in much better shape, and this same person will have taken one step further toward better health. One common side effect of a cleanse is loss of weight.

The last parts of me that can be damaged are the colon and rectum. Terry has mentioned this earlier. When he was on the SAD diet or standard American diet, he, too, would often have uncomfortable bowel movements that would cause bleeding at the rectum. Even before Terry began to gain knowledge about healthy diets, he knew that this condition could not be healthy and was concerned about the possibility of colon or rectal cancers. He is very thankful that this condition is no longer an issue. Terry has good bowel movements with his change of diet. Every once in a while, there will be an issue with a bowel movement, but it is rare. Everyone that has this same issue with bleeding should be concerned about serious health issues that can develop. This leads us to the next section of this book. I will make some basic recommendations on how to move toward better health and, *yes*, even healing of major diseases.

As a reader, you may expect this section of this book would be the longest. It will not be. The first sections of this book were written to help a person see how complicated I am and how easy it is to get me out of balance. Most individuals are born with a body that is in balance. It cannot be denied that genetics plays a role in our health. Terry will not get into this but will say that some individuals may be born with less than optimal health potential. This does not mean that a person that may have genetic weakness has an excuse for not being as healthy as he or she can be. It just means that if there is a family history of a weakness in an area of health, they must take extra care of me in that area. An example may be a family history of heart attacks. This person would get all the knowledge about building and maintaining a strong heart and cardiovascular system. This would have to start as early in life as possible. This would mean that parents would be the ones to start this program to strengthen any weakness in a family history.

A weakness in any part of my system can be strengthened and protected at any age. A person is never too old to work at strengthening one of my systems that may be weak either by genetics or mistakes made in taking care of me. Some weakened body issues may actually be the result of parent's lack of knowledge when it comes to the best care of infants. This leads to the most important statement made in the section of this book and maybe the whole book—I need to be given foods that are as close as they can be to the way God created them. It all starts with the very first meal a newborn will take into its body. Again, gaining knowledge is so important to making good decisions about health. Every new mother and father need to know the importance of colostrums for the newborn. I would suggest you google for the importance of colostrum. Colostrum is packed full of very necessary nutrients that a newborn infant needs for optimal health. It is true that babies that do not receive colostrum will live, but they are not given the chance to have the optimal level of health that they deserve. Terry mentioned earlier about the statement that the foods of today may keep us alive but will not allow us to be at optimal health. This is true with a newborn infant. Colostrum contains the following essential nutrients: antibodies, leukocytes, long chain polyunsaturated fatty acids, rich in vitamins and minerals, and three times the protein of mature milk. One site would be the following: www.mother-2-mother.com. Look under what is normal and then importance of colostrum. Terry heard a radio program produced by Dr. Robert Marshall, a very well-respected nutritionist, who had even recommended that older children that had not received colostrum at birth may benefit from taking a colostrum supplement to help improve their digestive system. There are very good colostrum supplements on the market that can help digestive disorders in adults. Again, Terry would encourage individuals to research the health advantages of a colostrum supplement.

Another issue that most expectant parents do not know about is the extreme importance of the health of the mother during pregnancy. It is, of course, understood that a healthy mother will give an infant the best chance for health, but most of us did not know that birth canal has a lot to do with the health of a newborn infant. As the infant moves through the birth canal, it takes into its digestive system the necessary good bacteria that will help with digestion and, most importantly, the immune system. It is a fact that cesarean-born babies do have more health issues that vaginally born babies. The reason for this is the lack of this good balance of bacteria in the digestive system. The health of the birth canal will, of course, have an influence on the newborn infant. If a pregnant woman insists on eating junk, drinking alcohol, smoking, or taking over-the-counter or illegal drugs, this infant will have less of a chance to be as healthy as they could be. In the womb, it is amazing how the unborn baby is protected from some of these abuses, but when this baby has to go through a polluted birth canal, his or her health is negatively affected. I would have had Terry write more about these subjects, but this book would be overwhelming. Again the purpose of this book is to spark a person's interest in gaining their own knowledge about how to gain health.

Once an individual gets past the nursing stage of life is when parents must play an important role in helping infants with food choices for health. It almost has to be a total family plan, which would include the grandparents. As Terry continues to talk to individuals about his excitement about health, he is amazed at how few people have an interest in eating healthy. When Terry has an opportunity to talk to parents with young children, he often tells them that he is very concerned about children. He knows that he and others his age had at least forty or fifty years of eating food without as many harmful additives and food lacking nutritional value. Most of his meals were prepared at home with real food—food as close to the way God created it as possible. In this current time frame, most food eaten by children is out of a box or fast food. As stated earlier, the food most individuals eat may keep them alive but not necessarily healthy.

Terry googled the following: *Food may keep us alive, but not healthy.* He was encouraged to come across a website by a Nathan Zehr. He has been a nutritionist for over thirty years. His website is www. nutritionsense.com. In a nutshell, it does a good job of explaining the importance of applied nutrition. It states "Nutrition, Simple and

Sensible". In this website, it states that the United States, according to the World Health Organization, has slipped from first to a tie with Serbia for thirty-seventh in regard to the world of health. This placing proves that the United States is not doing well in keeping its citizens well. Childhood diseases are rapidly growing. The two most alarming are diabetes and attention deficit disorder. Childhood diabetes and childhood obesity go hand in hand. Why is this happening? It is without a shadow of a doubt due to the lack of knowledge parents have concerning proper nutrition for children.

I, the body, would encourage readers to gain an understanding of how delicate I am and very easily damaged. It may take a few years or even a decade or two, but I will be damaged by poor nutrition. Terry has a theory about why most individuals are not concerned about what they eat. When my systems are very young, as in an infant, all my organs are fresh and in generally good condition. As a result, even if mistreated with poor nutrition, I am able to keep my digestive system and other organs working. If, however, this mistreatment continues, my organs begin to become stressed much earlier than they should, and they become weak. An example of this is childhood diabetes. When young children are allowed to let their taste buds dictate what tastes good, they begin to eat a lot of sugar and other sweets. This high level of sugar, as mentioned earlier in this book, causes my pancreas to be overwhelmed and not able to keep up with the demand for insulin. Lack of exercise and other poor diet choices add to the weakened pancreas. Because of this information, parents must gain knowledge as to how to take proper care of their young children and, of course, themselves. Most parents are young when they have their children. They are young enough to feel fairly healthy themselves, even though they are not taking the best care of themselves. There then comes the time when health issues begin to take place. These health issues, which may start out as fairly minor, may gradually get worse. It is at this point that the doctor's visits begin and pharmaceuticals begin to be taken. This is the norm in the

United States. There is very little awareness that knowing how to take better care of ourselves would be the best route to go.

Terry believes that this is changing. As he talks to anyone who will listen, and some will not, there are more and more individuals who are gaining some knowledge about different ways to take better care of themselves. Just within the last few years, there is more and more information that can be found on TV, cable, and radio that is trying to inform the public about taking care of me, the body. It is true that as there is a shift toward taking care of ourselves with more natural body-friendly products, there will be the greedy and dishonest individuals and companies that will try to take advantage of this movement. This is already happening. It will be up to you to really check out these products. That is why relying on a diet of healthy foods that are as close to the way God created them and finding the quality vitamins and supplements that will be needed to fill in some gaps are the keys to health. The gap that needs to be filled is minerals and vitamins. As written earlier, if foods, even organic, are not raised on high-quality, properly-taken-care-of soils, the plants that are grown on them will be lacking some of the microminerals and vitamins I need to stay truly healthy. As we try to end the writing of this book, Terry and I, the body, hope that there was enough information to help readers understand the importance of gaining as much knowledge as possible. This knowledge can help you stay as healthy as possible. It will help you keep your family members healthy. Even if there are inherited family weaknesses, that does not mean you have to give in to them. You may have to work harder to make decisions, but it can be done.

To help you with your search, we have decided to give you a start. Following is a list of suggestions for you to search.

Dr. Joseph Mercola
Dr. Richard Gerhauser
Dr. Glenn Rothfeld.
Dr. Mark Stengler
Health Science Institute
Natural News [Health Ranger Mike Adams]
Dr. Gary Null
Dr. Bruce West's Health Alert

POSSIBLE CANCER FIGHTERS OR CURES

Graviola
Essiac Tea
High dose IVs of vitamin C, B17, or other vitamin or supplement.

www.cancertutor.com/vitaminc.ivc/

Printed and bound by PG in the USA

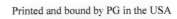

USA2019PGIL